Me, My Family and Friends

Pam Schiller

Special Needs Adaptations by Clarissa Willis

Acknowledgments

I would like to thank the following people for their contributions to this book. The special needs adaptations were written by Clarissa Willis. The CD is arranged by Patrick

Clarissa Willis

Patrick Brennan

Richele Bartkowiak

Brennan, and performed by Richele Bartkowiak and Patrick Brennan. It was engineered and mixed by Jeff Smith at Southwest Recordings. —Pam Schiller

Books written by Pam Schiller

The Bilingual Book of Rhymes, Songs, Stories, and Fingerplays, with Rafael Lara-Alecio and Beverly J. Irby

The Complete Book of Activities, Games, Stories, Props, Recipes, and Dances, with Jackie Silberg

The Complete Book of Rhymes, Songs, Poems, Fingerplays, and Chants, with Jackie Silberg

The Complete Daily Curriculum for Early Childhood: Over 1200 Easy Activities to Support Multiple Intelligences and Learning Styles, with Pat Phipps

The Complete Resource Book: An Early Childhood Curriculum, with Kay Hastings

The Complete Resource Book for Infants: Over 700 Experiences for Children From Birth to 18 Months

The Complete Resource Book for Toddlers and Twos: Over 2000 Experiences and Ideas

Count on Math: Activities for Small Hands and Lively Minds, with Lynne Peterson

Creating Readers: Over 1000 Games, Activities, Tongue Twisters, Fingerplays, Songs, and Stories to Get Children Excited About Reading

Do You Know the Muffin Man?, with Thomas Moore

The Instant Curriculum, Revised, with Joan Rosanno

The Practical Guide to Quality Child Care, with Patricia Carter Dyke

Start Smart: Building Brain Power in the Early Years

The Values Book, with Tamera Bryant

Where Is Thumbkin?, with Thomas Moore

CD INSIDE!

ME, My Family and Friends

26 Songs and Over 300 Activities for Young Children

Pam Schiller

Gryphon House, Inc.
Beltsville, Maryland

Me, My Family and Friends

© 2006 Pam Schiller
Printed in the United States of America.

Illustrations: Deborah Johnson
Cover Photograph: Getty Images, ©2005.

Published by Gryphon House, Inc.
10726 Tucker Street, Beltsville, MD 20705
301.595.9500; 301.595.0051 (fax); 800.638.0928 (toll-free)

Visit us on the web at www.ghbooks.com

 Gryphon House is a member of the Green Press Initiative, a nonprofit program dedicated to supporting publishers in their efforts to reduce their use of fiber sourced forests. For further information visit www.greenpressinitiative.org

Library of Congress Cataloging-in-Publication Data
Schiller, Pamela Byrne.
   Me, my family and friends / Pam Schiller ; illustrations, Deborah Johnson.
      p. cm.
   Includes bibliographical references (p.   ) and index.
   ISBN-13: 978-0-87659-042-3
   ISBN-10: 0-87659-042-3
 1. Music--Instruction and study--Juvenile. 2. Language arts (Early childhood)--Activity programs. 3. Children's songs. 4. Early childhood education--Activity programs. I. Johnson, Deborah, ill. II. Title.
   MT920.S42 2006
   372.87'044--dc22
                                                    2006010625

Table of Contents

Before serving food to children, be aware of children's food allergies and sensitivities, as well as any religious or cultural practices that exclude certain foods. Be sure to incorporate this information into your daily planning.

Introduction

Music in the Early Years

Music is a universal language, and singing is a hallmark of the early childhood classroom. Children love to sing. Teachers love to sing. Age and culture makes no difference.

Singing songs enriches thematic content, supports literacy concepts, and optimizes memory and learning. Add extensions of classroom activities, including modifications for special needs and English language learner populations, and it's a perfect package. *My, My Family and Friends* is one of eight thematic CD/book sets that offer all of these resources in one package.

Thematic Content

Me, My Family and Friends draws on typical early childhood themes: Physical Me, Thinking Me, Feelings, My Senses, Family, Friends, Farm, Things I Like, and Humor. Read the lyrics to the songs and decide which songs fit best in your curriculum.

Each song is accompanied by a list of facts titled "Did You Know?" These facts provide background information about the song, interesting facts about the topic or lyrics, historical information, or some form of trivia you might use as a springboard to discussion. This feature will save you hours of research and adds significantly to the value of the song.

Literacy Concepts

Young children need experiences that allow them to develop and practice basic literacy skills, such as listening, oral language development, phonological awareness, letter knowledge, print awareness, and comprehension. Suggestions for using the songs in *Me, My Family and Friends* as a springboard for teaching these literacy skills accompany every title. Below is a definition for each literacy skill and the sub-skills they encompass.

❑ **Listening:** the development of age-appropriate attention span, as well as the ability to listen for a variety of purposes; for example, details, directions, and sounds.

❑ **Oral Language Development:** the acquisition of vocabulary, the fine-tuning of grammar, and the increase in sentence length and complexity.

○ **Phonological Awareness:** sensitivity to the sounds of language. Phonological awareness begins with babbling and cooing and goes all the way through the understanding of sound and symbol relationships and decoding. The skills in the higher end of the phonological awareness continuum--sound and symbol relationship and decoding—are appropriate for children who are age five or older.

○ **Segmentation:** the breaking apart of words by syllable or letter; for example, children clap the breaks in the word *di-no-saur.*

○ **Rhyme:** words that sound alike. The ending sound of the words is the same, but the initial consonant sound is different, for example, *cat* and *hat* or *rake* and *cake.*

○ **Alliteration:** the repetition of a consonant sound in a series of words; for example, Peter Piper picked a peck of pickled peppers. Children need to be able to hear the repetition of the /p/ sound, but do not need to identify that the sound is made by the letter "p".

○ **Onomatopoeia:** words that imitate the sound they are describing; for example, *pitter-patter, moo, quack, beep,* and so on.

○ **Letter Knowledge:** the visual recognition of each letter of the alphabet, both lowercase and uppercase.

○ **Print Awareness:** the understanding that print has many functions; for example, telling a story, making a list, as part of signs, in news articles, in recipes, and so on. It is also the awareness that print moves left to right and top to bottom.

○ **Comprehension:** the internalization of a story or a concept.

Optimizing Memory and Learning

Singing boosts memory and keeps the brain alert. Increased memory and alertness optimize the potential for learning. When we sing we generally feel good. That sense of well-being causes the brain to release endorphins into the blood stream and those endorphins act as a memory fixative. When we sing we automatically increase our oxygen intake, which, in turn, increases our alertness. Scientific research has validated what early childhood professionals know intuitively—that singing has a positive effect on learning.

Expanding Children's Learning With Activities

Using songs as a springboard for classroom activities is a great way to bring the lyrics of the song into a meaningful context for children. Tracing hands and decorating them with fingerprints after singing "Where Is Thumbkin?" reinforces and creates meaningful context for the children's fingers and hands. Making Happy Face Puppets, creating a Happy Face snack, dancing a happy dance, discussing things that make us happy, and drawing happy pictures after singing "If You're Happy and You Know It" helps children better understand the concept of happiness.

Reading a book about being happy after singing about being happy also helps expand children's understanding. Literature selections are provided for each song. Integrating the teaching of themes and skills with songs, literature, and multidisciplinary activities provides a comprehensive approach for helping children recognize the patterns and the interconnected relationships of what they are learning.

Throughout the book, questions to ask children appear in italics. These questions are intended to help children think and reflect on what they have learned. This reflective process optimizes the opportunity for children to apply the information and experiences they have encountered.

Modifications

Suggestions for children with special needs and suggestions for English language learners accompany the song activities when appropriate. These features allow teachers to use the activities with diverse populations. All children love to sing and the benefits apply to all!

Special Needs

The inclusion of children with disabilities in preschool and child care programs is increasingly common. Parents, teachers, and researchers have found that children benefit in many ways from integrated programs that are designed to meet the needs of all children. Many children with disabilities, however, need accommodations to participate successfully in the general classroom.

Included in the extensions and activities for each song are adaptations for children with special needs. These adaptations allow *all* children to experience the song and related activities in a way that will maximize their learning opportunities. The adaptations are specifically for children who have needs in the following areas:

○ sensory integration
○ distractibility
○ hearing loss
○ spatial organization
○ language, receptive and expressive
○ fine motor coordination
○ cognitive challenges

The following general strategies from Kathleen Bulloch (2003) are for children who have difficulty listening and speaking.

Difficulty	Adaptations/Modifications/Strategies
Listening	○ State the objective—provide a reason for listening ○ Use a photo card ○ Give explanations in small, discrete steps ○ Be concise with verbal information: "Evan, please sit," instead of "Evan, would you please sit down in your chair?" ○ Provide visuals ○ Have the child repeat directions ○ Have the child close his eyes and try to visualize the information ○ Provide manipulative tasks ○ When giving directions to the class, leave a pause between each step so the child can carry out the process in her mind ○ Shorten the listening time required ○ Pre-teach difficult vocabulary and concepts
Verbal Expression	○ Provide a prompt, such as beginning the sentence for the child or giving a picture cue ○ Accept an alternate form of information-sharing, such as artistic creation, photos, charade or pantomime, and demonstration ○ Ask questions that require short answers ○ Specifically teaching body and language expression ○ First ask questions at the information level—giving facts and asking for facts back ○ Wait for children to respond; don't call on the first child to raise his hand ○ Have the child break in gradually by speaking in smaller groups and then in larger groups

English Language Learners

Strategies for English language learners are also provided to maximize their learning.

The following are general strategies for working with English language learners (Gray, Fleischman, 2004-05):

❍ **Keep the language simple.** Speak simply and clearly. Use short, complete sentences in a normal tone of voice. Avoid using slang, idioms, or figures of speech.
❍ **Use actions and illustrations to reinforce oral statements.** Appropriate prompts and facial expressions help convey meaning.
❍ **Ask for completion, not generation.** Ask children to choose answers from a list or to complete a partially finished sentence. Encourage children to use language as much as possible to gain confidence over time.
❍ **Model correct usage and judiciously correct errors.** Use corrections to positively reinforce children's use of English. When English language learners make a mistake or use awkward language, they are often attempting to apply what they know about their first language to English. For example, a Spanish-speaking child may say, "It fell from me," a direct translation from Spanish, instead of "I dropped it."
❍ **Use visual aids.** Present classroom content and information in a way that engages children—by using graphic organizers (word web, story maps, KWL charts), photographs, concrete materials, and graphs, for example.

Involving English Language Learners in Music Activities

Music is a universal language that draws people together. For English language learners, music can be a powerful vehicle for language learning and community-building. Music and singing are important to second language learners for many reasons, including:

❍ The rhythms of music help children hear the sounds and intonation patterns of a new language.
❍ Musical lyrics and accompanying motions help children learn new vocabulary.
❍ Repetitive patterns of language in songs help children internalize the sentence structure of English.
❍ Important cultural information is conveyed to young children in the themes of songs.

Strategies for involving English language learners in music activities vary according to the children's level of proficiency in the English language.

Level of Proficiency	Strategies
Beginning English Language Learners	o Keep the child near you and model motions as you engage in group singing. o Use hand gestures, movements, and signs as often as possible to accompany song lyrics, making sure to tie a specific motion to a specific word. o Refer to real objects in the environment that are named in a song. o Stress the intonation, sounds, and patterns in language by speaking the lyrics of the song while performing actions or referring to objects in the environment. o Use simple, more common vocabulary. For example, use *round* instead of *circular*.
Intermediate-Level English Language Learners	o Say the song before singing it, so children can hear the words and rhythms of the lyrics. o Use motions, gestures, and signs to help children internalize the meaning of song lyrics. Be sure the motion is tied clearly to the associated word. o Throughout the day, repeat the language patterns found in songs in various activities. o Stress the language patterns in songs, and pause as children fill in the blanks. o Adapt the patterns of song, using familiar vocabulary.
Advanced English Language Learners	o Use visuals to cue parts of a song. o Use graphic organizers to introduce unfamiliar information. o Use synonyms for words heard in songs to expand children's vocabulary. o Develop vocabulary through description and comparison. For example, it is *round* like a circle. It is *circular*. o Encourage children to make up new lyrics for songs.

How to Use This Book

Use the 26 songs on the *Me, My Family and Friends* CD (included with this book) and the related activities in this book to enhance themes in your curriculum, or use them independently. Either way you have a rich treasure chest of creative ideas for your classroom.

The eight-package collection provides more than 200 songs, a perfect combination of the traditional best-loved children's songs and brand new selections created for each theme. Keep a song in your heart and put joy in your teaching!

Bibliography

Bulloch, K. 2003. *The mystery of modifying: Creative solutions.* Huntsville, TX: Education Service Center, Region VI.

Cavallaro, C. & M. Haney. 1999. *Preschool inclusion.* Baltimore, MD: Paul H. Brookes Publishing Company.

Gray, T. and S. Fleischman. Dec. 2004-Jan. 2005. "Research matters: Successful strategies for English language learners." *Educational Leadership,* 62, 84-85.

Hanniford, C. 1995. *Smart moves: Why learning is not all in your head.* Arlington, VA: Great Ocean Publications, p. 146.

LeDoux, J. 1993. "Emotional memory systems in the brain." *Behavioral and Brain Research,* 58.

Tabors, P. 1997. *One child, two languages: Children learning English as a second language.* Baltimore, MD: Paul H. Brookes Publishing Company.

ME, MY FAMILY AND FRIENDS

Songs and Activities

Magic

When I was young I thought the stars were made for wishing on,
And every hole inside a tree might hide a leprechaun.
And houses all had secret rooms, if one could find the door.
But who believes in magic, anymore?

Chorus:
Magic is the sun that makes a rainbow out of rain.
Magic keeps the dream alive to try and try again.
Magic is the love that stays when good friends have to leave.
I do believe in magic—I believe.

Growing up, the grownups said someday I'd wake to find
That magic's just a childhood dream I'd have to leave behind
Like clothes that would no longer fit or toys that I'd ignore.
I'd not believe in magic, anymore.

(Chorus)

Now that I am grown I found that much to my surprise,
Magic did not fade away, it took a new disguise,
A child, a friend, a smile, a song, the courage to stand tall.
I do believe in magic after all.

Magic is the sun that makes a rainbow out of rain.
Magic keeps the dream alive to try and try again.
Magic is the love that stays when good friends have to leave.
I do believe in magic. Do you believe in magic?
I do believe in magic—I believe.

Vocabulary

believe	hole
courage	ignore
disguise	leprechaun
fade	magic
friends	rainbow
growing up	stand tall
grown	star
grown-ups	sun

Theme Connections

Growing Things
Magic
Me

Special Needs Adaptation: Often children with special needs have difficulty understanding the difference between what is real and what is not. Explain that magic can be a way to entertain others, but that magic tricks should only be attempted with an adult present.

Did You Know?

- Several well known individuals have been magicians, including Johnny Carson, Jimmy Stewart, Woody Allen, Jason Alexander, Cary Grant, Fred Astaire, John Denver, and George Herbert Walker Bush.
- Pulling a rabbit from a hat is a classic symbol of magic, yet is rarely a part of a magician's show. By some accounts, the idea of pulling a rabbit from a hat was part of a publicity stunt. Created by a British magician, the effect capitalized on the public's interest in a woman who claimed to have given birth to a litter of rabbits.

○ Some famous magicians were physically challenged. Eliaser Bamberg had only one leg (and he used his false leg to hide magic items). George Kirkland, who was blind since birth, entertained Britons in the late 1800's. Today, Argentina's Rene Levante is famous for his amazing card magic, even though he has only one arm.

○ David Copperfield is the most highly paid magician of all time. He is on the Fortune 500 list.

Literacy Links

Oral Language

○ Talk about growing up. *How are grownups different from children? How are they alike? What does it mean to be grown up?*

○ Teach the children the American Sign Language sign for *magic*.

○ Talk about magic. *How does magic work? What magic things do you know about?*

○ Ask the children what wish they would make if they made a wish on a star. Teach them "Star Light, Star Bright."

Star Light, Star Bright
Star light, star bright,
First star I've seen tonight.
I wish I may, I wish I might
Have this wish I wish tonight.

magic

Curriculum Connections

Art

○ Provide lemon juice in squirt bottles. Invite the children to spray a design on dark colors of construction paper and then place their picture in the sun to dry. *What happens?*

Discovery

○ Provide prisms. Suggest that the children hold the prisms in a sunny window to make rainbows.

Dramatic Play

○ Fill the center with clothes, some of which are too small for the children. Have the children try things on to see what fits and what doesn't. Talk about growing out of clothes. Remind the children that they were once babies and wore very small clothes.

Book Corner

Games

❍ Invite the children to play Find the Leprechaun. Use a leprechaun doll or draw a leprechaun on a piece of poster board. Hide the leprechaun under one of three small boxes. Move the boxes around and ask the children to guess which box is hiding the leprechaun.

Science

❍ Provide magnetic or felt letters. Have the children spell *magic* by placing the letters on black or blue construction paper. Place their papers outside in the sun for a few hours. Have the children remove the letters to reveal a surprise underneath. *What does the word on the paper say?*

❍ Invite the children to grow a Magic Crystal Garden (page 103).

Snack

❍ Provide a carbonated clear soda and raisins. Encourage the children to drop raisins into their soda and watch the magic. The bubbles in the soda will cause the raisins to rise to the surface and then magically drop again (when the bubbles that are surrounding them pop).

Writing

❍ Print *magic* on chart paper. Provide magic slates. Invite the children to write *magic* on the magic slates and then lift the page to make the word disappear.

Home Connection

❍ Suggest that children interview the adult members of their families about their favorite childhood memories. Discuss their interviews the next day in morning circle.

Where Is Thumbkin?

Vocabulary

here	Thumbkin
Middleman	today
Pinky	very well
Pointer	where
Ring man	

Theme Connections

Me
My Senses
Parts of the Body

Where is Thumbkin?
Where is Thumbkin?
Here I am. Here I am.
How are you today, sir?
Very well, I thank you.
Run away. Run away.

Additional verses:
Where is Pointer?
Where is Middleman?
Where is Ring man?
Where is Pinky?

Did You Know?

❍ The muscles that power our fingers are strong—so strong that they can actually support our body weight.

❍ On winter nights, many people suffer from cold hands or feet. This common response allows mammals to conserve body heat when temperatures are low. Polar animals take this to extremes—temperatures in their extremities fall to near freezing so their body core stays toasty.

❍ There's more to good hand washing than you think, so take your time and do it right. Rub your hands vigorously with soapy water, which takes soil and oily dirt away from the skin. The lather traps the dirt and germs so they can be rinsed away. Lather with soap for at least 10 seconds. Wash the front and back of hands, between fingers, and under nails. Rinse hands well under warm, running water and dry them completely with a clean towel.

❍ Encourage children to wash hands before eating, after playing outdoors, after playing with pets, after using the bathroom, and after blowing their noses. Even though hands might look clean, they often carry germs or microorganisms that are capable of causing disease.

Literacy Links

Oral Language

❍ Discuss the different names for each of the fingers.
❍ Talk about the ways we use our fingers.

○ Teach the children the American Sign Language signs for *hand* and *finger* (page 115).
○ Teach the children "Five Little Fingers."

Five Little Fingers
One little finger standing on its own. (hold up index finger)
Two little fingers, now they're not alone. (hold up middle finger)
Three little fingers, happy as can be. (hold up ring finger)
Four little fingers go walking down the street. (hold up all fingers)
Five little fingers, this one is a thumb. (hold up four fingers and thumb)
Wave bye-bye 'cause now we are done. (wave bye-bye)

○ Sing *Where Is Thumbkin?* using family member names for the fingers. Use the words Mommy, Daddy, brother, sister, and baby instead of finger names.

> **English Language Learner Strategy:** Encourage a family member to talk to the class. Have the child introduce his or her family member to his or her friends.

Print Awareness
○ Print *Where Is Thumbkin?* on chart paper. Point out the question mark at the end of the words. Tell the children that this symbol is a question mark and that it is used when one asks a question.

Curriculum Connections

Art
○ Invite the children to finger paint. Discuss their fingers as they work. How do they use their thumbs when painting? Invite the children to make fingerprints.

Discovery
○ Have the children trace their hands. Provide an ink pad and encourage the children to make a fingerprint on each finger of the traced hand. Have the children look at their fingerprints with a magnifying glass.

inkpad
fingerprints

> **Special Needs Adaptation:** Children with certain disabilities, especially autism spectrum disorder or sensory integration issues, may be unwilling or have difficulty participating in this activity. As an alternative, invite the child to look at another child's fingerprints.

Dramatic Play

❍ Photocopy, color, cut out, and laminate the Finger Puppets (page 108). Encourage the children to play with the puppets. Talk about using their fingers as legs.

❍ Provide rings and gloves for the children to explore.

Fine Motor

❍ Provide playdough for the children. Discuss how they use their hands with the dough.

Math

❍ Make rings from pipe cleaners or, if available, use real rings. Encourage the children to practice one-to-one correspondence by matching one ring to each finger on their hands. *How many rings do you have on your hand?*

❍ Have the children search for someone with hands larger than theirs. Do they think to measure their hand against your hand?

Music and Movement

❍ Encourage the children to sing songs about fingers such as "Open, Shut Them" (page 55) and chants about fingers "Thelma Thumb" (page 100). Teach them fingerplays (page 101).

Sand and Water

❍ Provide eyedroppers and containers. Encourage the children to use the eyedroppers to fill the containers. *Which fingers do you use to work the eyedroppers?*

Snacks

❍ Offer finger foods for snack, such as crackers, carrots, marshmallows, and/or cheese cubes. Discuss other finger foods. *Why do we call them finger foods?*

Writing

❍ Print *thumb* on index cards. Provide fingerpaint. Encourage the children to cover the letters with thumbprints.

Home Connection

❍ Encourage the children to teach "Where Is Thumbkin?" to their families.

Eyes, Nose, Fingers, and Toes by Judy Hindley

Hand, Hand, Fingers, Thumb by Al Perkins

Here Are My Hands by Bill Martin, Jr.

Ten Little Fingers by Annie Kubler

SONGS AND ACTIVITIES

Are You Sleeping?

Are you sleeping,
Are you sleeping,
Brother John, Brother John?
Morning bells are ringing.
Morning bells are ringing.
Ding! Dong! Ding!
Ding! Dong! Ding!
(Repeat)

Vocabulary

Brother John
ding
dong
morning bells
ringing
sleeping

Theme Connections

Me
Nighttime

Did You Know?

○ We spend one third of our life sleeping. Children up to age 10 should sleep 10 hours each night.
○ The body rests during sleep. The brain, however, remains active, getting "recharged," while still controlling many body functions, including breathing. When we sleep, we typically drift between two sleep states, REM (rapid eye movement) and non-REM, in 90-minute cycles. Non-REM sleep has four stages with distinct features, ranging from stage one, drowsiness, when one can be easily awakened, to "deep sleep," stages three and four, when awakenings are more difficult and where the most positive and restorative effects of sleep occur. However, even in the deepest non-REM sleep, our minds can still process information. REM sleep is an active sleep where dreams occur, breathing and heart rate increase and become irregular, muscles relax, and eyes move back and forth under the eyelids.
(Source: The National Sleep Foundation, Washington, DC)

Literacy Links

Oral Language
○ Teach the children the American Sign Language sign for *goodnight* (page 115).
○ Teach the children "Be Very Quiet."

> **Be Very Quiet**
> *Shhh, be very quiet.*   *Close your sleepy little eyes.*
> *Shhh, be very still.*   *Shhh, be very quiet.*
> *Fold your busy little hands,*

❍ Discuss sleeping habits. Ask children what they do to get ready for bed. Discuss bedtime routines.

✓ **Special Needs Adaptation:** Ask the child's family to tell you about his bedtime routine. Talk to the child about his routine. Explain that going to bed at night can be a fun time. Discuss why it is important to be quiet when others are resting or sleeping. Invite the child to whisper and role play how to act when someone is sleeping.

Phonological Awareness
❍ Sing the song substituting "zing, zong, zing" for "ding, dong, ding." *Does it change the song?* Try other consonant substitutions.

Print Awareness
❍ Print the song on chart paper. Move your hand under the words as you sing the song. Point out the left-to-right and top-to-bottom progression of the words. Point out the question mark. Tell the children that a question mark indicates asking a question.

Curriculum Connections

Art
❍ Provide drawing paper and crayons. Have the children draw a sleepy time picture.

Discovery
❍ Provide a variety of bells, such as a kitchen timer, jingle bells, tambourines, and service bells, for the children to explore.

Dramatic Play
❍ Provide baby dolls and encourage the children to put the babies to bed. Suggest they rock the babies and sing lullabies to the babies.

Gross Motor
❍ Use masking tape to create a throw line. Provide a beanbag and a service bell. Encourage the children to toss the beanbag in an attempt to ring the service bell.

Book Corner

Listening

○ Provide large-sized jingle bells and three different types of containers, such as a tin can, a plastic bottle, and a cardboard box. Encourage the children to place a bell in each container and then shake them to determine if the type of container changes the sound.

Math

○ Provide ten wiggle eyes. Have the children hold the eyes in their hands and then drop them onto a blue plastic plate or blue sheet of construction paper. Encourage the children to match the eyes that land facing up (wakeful eyes) and the eyes that land facing down (sleeping eyes) one-to-one to see if there are more wakeful eyes or sleeping eyes.

○ Make Bell Blocks. Place jingle bells inside clean half-pint milk cartons. Fill one carton with one jingle bell, put two jingle bells in the next carton, and so on up to five bells. Square off the lids and tape each carton closed. Have the children ring the blocks and then place the blocks in order from the block with the softest sound to the block with the loudest sound.

Music

○ Teach the children lullabies, such as "Rockabye, Baby" and "Bye Baby Bunting."

Writing

○ Trace around magnetic letters on drawing paper to write *ding, dong, ding*. Invite the children to place magnetic letters on top of the letters.

○ Print *Quiet* on a sheet of drawing paper. Provide crayons and paper and encourage the children to copy the word.

Home Connections

○ Have the children look at home for alarm clocks. How many do they find? Make a graph of the number of clocks in each home when the children return to school.

○ Suggest that the children ask their families what lullabies were sung to them when they were little.

Make New Friends

Vocabulary

friends
gold
keep
new
old
silver

Theme Connections

Colors
Friends

Make new friends,
But keep the old.
One is silver
And the other's gold.
(Repeat two more times.)

Did You Know?

○ International Friendship Day, the first Sunday in August, is a time to recognize your friends and their contribution to your life. Friendship helps to bring peace and caring to the globe, which is a great reason to celebrate!

○ Friends come in all shapes, sizes, and ages: school friends, work colleagues, siblings, partners, parents, family members, pets, and neighbors.

Literacy Links

Oral Language

○ Talk about friendship. *What does it mean to be a friend?*

○ Teach the children the American Sign Language sign for *friend* (page 115).

Phonological Awareness

○ Print *old* on chart paper. Just below it print *gold*. Encourage the children to try adding other letters of the alphabet in front of *old* to create more words. For example, if you add a "b" you have *bold*. Read the list of words that you created, and then make sure the children understand that it is a list of rhyming words.

Curriculum Connections

Art
❍ Provide paper, paintbrushes, and gold and silver tempera paint. Invite the children to paint with the silver and gold tempera paint.

Cooking
❍ Invite the children to follow the Friendship Donut Rebus Recipe (page 104). **Safety Note**: Keep the children away from the fryer. Only the teacher should drop the donuts in the grease.

> **English Language Learner Strategy:** Take a photograph of each step as the children make their friendship donuts. Record the directions on a tape. Place the photographs and the tape in the Listening Center. Have the children put the photos in sequence as they listen to the tape.

Games
❍ Make a Find a Friend Game. Take photographs of the children and copy the photographs to make a set of two for each photograph. Glue one set of photos inside a colorful folder in a board game-style pathway. Cut the second set of photos out and store them in a zipper-closure bag. Invite the children to match the photos in the bag to those in the folder.

Gross Motor
❍ Teach the children to do Back-to-Back Lifts. Have children select a partner and sit back to back. Show them how to lock elbows, press against one another, and stand up.

Book Corner

Best Friends by
Steven Kellogg
Chester's Way by
Kevin Henkes
Ginger by Charlotte
Voake
My Friends by Taro
Gomi
*Will You Be My
Friend? A Bunny
and Bird Story* by
Nancy Tafuri

Language

O Make Friendship Puzzles. Take photos of the children. Photocopy and enlarge the photos and laminate the copies. Cut the laminated copies into puzzle pieces and invite the children to work the puzzles. Talk with the children about how the puzzle pieces fit together.

Library

O Suggest that friends read a book together.

Music and Movement

O Play marching music. Invite the children to select a partner and then march around the classroom in a Friendship March.

  Special Needs Adaptation: Some children with special needs have difficulty making friends. Adapt this activity by helping the child select a partner. Before the activity, select someone to be his marching partner and talk to that child. Invite the peer to be a peer buddy and explain that the child with special needs may need to walk more slowly or not walk at all. For children unable to walk or march due to a motor or physical limitation, they can participate by waving a scarf or beating a drum.

Writing

O Invite the children to make a card for a friend.

O See pages 40 and 43 for more activities about friends.

Home Connection

O Send each child's photo puzzles home and suggest they show their family members how to work their puzzle.

If You're Happy and You Know It

If you're happy and you know it, clap your hands. *(clap, clap)*
If you're happy and you know it, clap your hands. *(clap, clap)*
If you're happy and you know it, then your face will surely show it.
If you're happy and you know it, clap your hands. *(clap, clap)*

Additional verses:
…stomp your feet… *(stomp, stomp)*
…shout hooray! … *(hooray! hooray!)*
…do all three… *(clap, clap; stomp, stomp, hooray! hooray!)*

Vocabulary

clap
face
feet
hands
happy
hooray
know
shout
show
stomp
three

Theme Connections

Feelings
Parts of the Body

Did You Know?

- ❍ Facial muscles are attached directly to the skin (unlike anywhere else on the body) allowing us to perform an extensive array of facial expressions.
- ❍ Facial expressions reflect our emotions.
- ❍ People rarely see their own profiles. When they do, it's in a reflection, therefore reversed.
- ❍ Face facts:
  - ○ Eyelashes keep grit and glare from our eyes.
  - ○ Babies' eyes are adult size at birth.
  - ○ The thinnest skin on the body is the eyelid. The thickest? The soles of feet.
  - ○ Egyptians had many of the same cosmetics that we use today.

Literacy Links

Comprehension

- ❍ Read the action story, "The Many Faces of Me" (page 101). Invite children to think of other faces and what things cause them to make the faces mentioned in the story.

> ✓ **English Language Learner Strategy:** Read the story while the child looks into the mirror. Stop at each expression and demonstrate the expression while the child watches in the mirror. Ask the child to mimic your expressions.

Letter Knowledge

❍ Print *happy* on chart paper. Have the children identify the letters. *Which letter is in the word twice?*

Oral Language

❍ Teach the children the American Sign Language signs for *happy* and *sad* (pages 116-117).

❍ Talk about emotions and the things that cause them. Have children demonstrate different facial expressions to convey different emotions.

Oral Language/Comprehension

❍ Change the words to the song to reflect other emotions and ways to show them. For example, you might say "If you're angry and you know it say, 'I'm mad.'" Sing "If You're Happy, Laugh Out Loud" (page 98).

happy

Curriculum Connections

Art

❍ Invite the children to paint happy faces. Cut easel paper into circles and provide easel paint and markers for the children to add facial features.

❍ Encourage the children to draw a picture of something that makes them happy.

Construction

❍ Invite the children to make Happy Face Puppets. Give each child a paper plate, craft stick, strips of yarn, and markers. Have the children draw happy faces on their plates and then glue the yarn on the plate for hair. Then have them attach the plates to craft sticks to create puppets.

Games

❍ Make two photocopies of the Happy Face Match Up Patterns (page 109). Color them and cut them out. Give the children the cards and suggest they play Happy Face Concentration.

Book Corner

English Language Learner Strategy: Pair a proficient English speaker with an English language learner. Review the game directions with them before starting the game. Stress game vocabulary, such as *turn over, your turn, my turn, they match,* and *they don't match.*

Gross Motor

❍ Provide large-size bubble wrap and encourage the children to stomp the bubbles.

Math

❍ Suggest that the children make up clapping patterns. Record their patterns and then see if they can identify their pattern when they hear it played back.

Music and Movement

❍ Teach the children to perform the "Happy Snappy Clappy Tappy Dance." Chant the rhyme and suit actions to the words.

> **Happy Snappy Clappy Tappy Dance** by Pam Schiller
> Snap, snap, snap your fingers and turn yourself around.
> Tap, tap, tap your foot in a circle on the ground.
> Clap, clap, clap your hands—way up high and then down low.
> Tap, tap, tap your foot, tap it heel and toe.
> Smile a great big happy smile,
> And dance this happy dance in style.

Snack

❍ Have the children follow the Happy Face Rebus Recipe (page 105) to create Happy Face Cookies.

Writing

❍ Print *happy* on chart paper. Invite the children to use magnetic letters to spell happy.

Home Connection

❍ Suggest that the children talk with their families about things that make them happy.

S-M-I-L-E

Vocabulary

bubble
grin
laugh
smile
trouble
vanish

Theme Connections

Expressions
Feelings
Humor

(Tune: Battle Hymn of the Republic)
It isn't any trouble just to S-M-I-L-E.
It isn't any trouble just to S-M-I-L-E.
So smile when you're in trouble,
It will vanish like a bubble,
If you'll only take the trouble just to S-M-I-L-E.

It isn't any trouble just to L-A-U-G-H.
It isn't any trouble just to L-A-U-G-H.
So laugh when you're in trouble,
It will vanish like a bubble,
If you'll only take the trouble just to L-A-U-G-H.

It isn't any trouble just to G-R-I-N, grin.
It isn't any trouble just to G-R-I-N, grin.
So grin when you're in trouble,
It will vanish like a bubble,
If you'll only take the trouble just to G-R-I-N, grin!

Ha! Ha! Ha! Ha! Ha! Ha!
Ha! Ha! Ha! Ha! Ha! Ha! Ha!
Ha! Ha! Ha! Ha! Ha! Ha!
Ha! Ha! Ha! Ha! Ha! Ha! Ha!
Ha! Ha! Ha! Ha! Ha! Ha!
Ha! Ha! Ha! Ha! Ha! Ha!
Ha! Ha! Ha! Ha! Ha! Ha! Ha!
Ha! Ha!

Did You Know?

○ On average, children laugh 400 times per day while adults laugh only 15 times per day! You can't laugh too much, so finding ways to increase laughter for both children and adults is a worthy pursuit.

○ Laughter is a form of release. It allows us to rid ourselves of negative emotions that cause harmful chemical effects on the body (Berk & Tan 1996).

○ Just like exercise, laughter has two stages—the arousal phase that increases the heart rate and the resolution phase that allows the heart to rest. Laughing can lower blood pressure, increase vascular flow, and boost the immune system. It gives the diaphragm, abdominal, respiratory system, and facial muscles a workout. Some people even use their arm, leg, and back muscles when laughing!

○ New studies show that humor stimulates regions of the brain known as reward centers. These reward centers release chemicals that play a vital role in the brain's pleasure and reward system. It appears that the brain feels rewarded by finding something funny. This lends credence to the idea that laughter is therapeutic—for some people it creates a natural high.

○ A person who studies laughter is called a *gelotologist*.
Berk, L, & S. Tan. 1996. "The Laughter-Immune Connection." Available from http://www.touchstarpro.com/laughbb3.html (17 April 1997).

Literacy Links

Listening
○ Read the story, "What Makes Me Laugh?" (page 102). After reading it, ask the children to name the funny things mentioned in the story.

Oral Language
○ Talk with the children about the ways that they show they are happy.
○ Teach the children the American Sign Language signs for *smile* and *laugh* (pages 116-117).
○ Read the poem, "What Makes Me Laugh?" (page 101). Challenge the children to add things to the list of things in the poem.

Phonological Awareness
○ Sing the last verse using *he-he* instead of *ha-ha*. Try singing it with all kinds of laughter expressions, such as *ha-ha*, *he-he*, and *ho-ho*, all at one time.

Phonological Awareness/Letter Knowledge
○ Print *he-he*, *ha-ha*, and *ho-ho* on chart paper. Have the children identify the letters. Say the words one at a time and ask the children to listen to the differences in these words that have only one letter changed.

smile

Curriculum Connections

Art
○ Invite the children to make Smile Posters. Print *SMILE* in bubble letters on sheets of art paper. Invite the children to decorate the letters with dots, stripes, and other patterns.

Games
○ Invite the children to play, "You Can't Make Me Laugh." Assign one child to be "IT." IT tries to make the other children laugh by doing silly antics. The first child who laughs becomes the next IT.

❍ Encourage the children to play a game of Tummy Ticklers. Have the children lie on the floor on their backs with their heads on someone else's tummy. Do something silly to make the children start laughing. What is making their heads jiggle? This activity should cause contagious laughing.

 Special Needs Adaptation: Demonstrate how to do Tummy Ticklers. Sometimes children will be more willing to participate if the activity is one in which they know what will happen. Explain that the game is for fun and do not force a child to participate if he is unwilling. For a child with severe disabilities or one with sensory integration issues, adapt the activity by inviting the child to place her hands on her own tummy and see how it feels when she laughs.

Library

❍ Place funny papers (comics) in the library center for the children to look at and "read."

Listening

❍ Provide a tape recorder. Invite the children to record their laughter. Can they identify their laughter when they play the tape?

Music

❍ Sing silly songs like "Catalina Magnalina" (page 34), "I Wish I Were" (page 85), "One Black Bear" (page 98), and "The Song That Never Ends" (page 99).

Writing

❍ Print *ha-ha*, *he-he*, and *ho-ho*, on chart paper. Invite the children to make the letters with playdough to spell the words.
❍ Have the children use magnetic letters or felt letters to spell *smile*, *grin*, and *laugh*.

Home Connection

❍ Encourage the children to spell *grin*, *laugh*, and *smile* for their families.

The Cat in the Hat by Dr. Seuss
Don't Make Me Laugh by James Stevenson
Giggle Belly by Page Sakelaris
Giggle, Giggle, Quack by Doreen Cronin
Green Eggs and Ham by Dr. Seuss
Toes Have Wiggles, Kids Have Giggles by Harriet Ziefert
Wacky Wednesday by Dr. Seuss

SONGS AND ACTIVITIES

Catalina Magnalina

She had a peculiar name but she
    wasn't to blame.
She got it from her mother who's
    the same, same, same.

Chorus:
Catalina Magnalina,
    Hootensteiner Bogentwiner
Hogan Logan Bogan was her
    name.

She had two peculiar eyes in
    her head.
One was purple and the other
    was red.

(Chorus)

She had two peculiar teeth in
    her mouth.
One pointed north and the other
    pointed south.

(Chorus)

She had two peculiar hairs on
    her chin.
One stuck out and the other
    stuck in.

(Chorus)

She had two feet like bathroom
    mats.
I forgot to ask her how they got
    like that.

(Chorus)

Catalina Magnalina,
    Hootensteiner Bogentwiner
Hogan Logan Bogan was her
    name.

Vocabulary

bathroom mats
blame
chin
eyes
feet
head
mother
mouth
name
north
peculiar
purple
red
same
south
stuck in
stuck out
teeth

Theme Connections

Humor
Rhyming Words

Did You Know?

❍ Humor is good for our bodies and good for
   our brains. Laughter increases the white blood cell activity in our bodies.
   White blood cells boost our immune system, which helps us fight off
   illnesses.

❍ Laughter also increases the chemicals in our body associated with memory
   and alertness. The increase of these chemicals, called endorphins, also
   reduces stress. Low stress enhances the brain's receptivity to learning.

❍ Humor is an important ingredient in the early childhood experiences. The
   more we laugh the more we learn, the happier we feel, and the healthier
   we stay.

Literacy Links

Oral Language/Comprehension
❍ Teach the children "Annie Mae" (page 97). Compare Catalina to Annie Mae.

Phonological Awareness
❍ Write Catalina's full name on a piece of chart paper. Find the rhyming words in her name.
❍ Encourage the children to create their own rhyming names, such as Silly Billy, Tabby Abby, and Carlos Starlos.

Curriculum Connections

Art
❍ Invite the children to draw a picture of Catalina.

Discovery
❍ Provide a compass and invite the children to locate north and south.

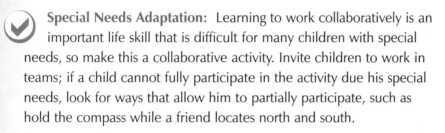 **Special Needs Adaptation:** Learning to work collaboratively is an important life skill that is difficult for many children with special needs, so make this a collaborative activity. Invite children to work in teams; if a child cannot fully participate in the activity due his special needs, look for ways that allow him to partially participate, such as hold the compass while a friend locates north and south.

Games
❍ Invite the children to play Rhyme or Reason. Give the children a word to start the game. Point to a child and ask that child to add either a rhyming word or an associated word to continue the game. For example, if you start the game with *sun*, the child might say *fun* to rhyme with your word or *moon* to provide a word that is associated with your word. After each child makes a contribution, she points to a new child to continue the game.

Book Corner

Gross Motor

○ Draw a 24" circle on bulletin board paper for Catalina's head. Draw her mouth, nose, and eyes. Give the children a purple beanbag and a red beanbag. Use masking tape to create a throw line. Have the children attempt to toss the red beanbag onto the red eye and the purple beanbag onto the purple eye.

Language

○ Make a name puzzle. Print *Catalina Magnalina* on a 4" x 18" strip of poster board. Print the letters far enough apart to allow you to cut a puzzle line between the letters. Laminate the strip and cut it into puzzle pieces.

Math

○ Write Catalina's full name on a piece of chart paper. Help the children count the letters in her name.

○ Make a graph that shows children's eye color. *Does anyone have purple or red eyes?*

Music

○ Sing rhyming word songs such as "Down by the Bay."

Snack

○ Invite the children to use the Catalina Magnalina Shakalina Rebus Recipe cards (page 106) to make Catalina shakes.

Writing

○ Print *Catalina Magnalina* on chart paper. Provide Scrabble tiles. Invite the children to use the letters to spell Catalina's name.

Home Connection

○ Suggest that children tell their families about Catalina Magnalina.

This Is Tiffany by Pam Schiller

Vocabulary

black
blue
bright
dress
favorite
friend
fuzzy
glad
new
pink
red
shirt
shoes
sweater

Theme Connections

Clothing
Colors

This is Tiffany over here.
She has on a bright blue dress.
This is Tiffany, our new friend.
We're so glad she's here.

This is Patrick over here.
He has on new black shoes.
This is Patrick, our new friend.
We're so glad he's here.

This is Carmen over here.
She has on a fuzzy pink sweater.
This is Carmen, our new friend.
We're so glad she's here.

This is Jonathan over here.
He has on his favorite red shirt.
This is Jonathan, our new friend.
We're so glad he's here.

Did You Know?

○ Children discover and learn about their world through play. Play develops imagination and creativity and gives children practice in social skills, such as waiting, taking turns, cooperating, and sharing things.

○ Children go through stages of play as they grow and mature. The stages of play are:

  ○ Solitary Play—A child is in a room full of other children, but he/she is playing alone and not paying attention to anyone.

  ○ Parallel Play—Children are playing next to each other, but they are not talking or doing the same activity.

  ○ Associative Play—Children are playing the same game, but they are not working together or connecting with one another.

  ○ Cooperative Play—Children are working together to play a game.

Literacy Links

Oral Language

❍ Sing the song several times, changing the clothing descriptions to match children in the room. Sing the song by humming the child's name but still providing clothing descriptions. Can the children guess who you are singing about?

❍ Talk about things we can do to help new friends feel welcome.

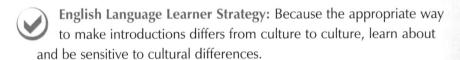 **Special Needs Adaptation:** Select one or two specific things that children do to make new friends feel welcome, such as sharing a toy or offering to play with the new friend. Many times, children with special needs don't know how to be a friend to others. Look for opportunities throughout the day to point out examples of things that children do to make others feel welcome. For a child who is nonverbal, look for nonverbal ways to make him feel welcome or ways he can make others feel welcome, such as using the sign for *hello* (page 116).

❍ Discuss the proper way to introduce a friend. Have the children demonstrate proper introductions.

English Language Learner Strategy: Because the appropriate way to make introductions differs from culture to culture, learn about and be sensitive to cultural differences.

Curriculum Connections

Art

❍ Provide easel paper and tempera paints. Have the children select a friend to paint with, using the same paper and paints.

Blocks

❍ Encourage children to find a friend to build with.

Fine Motor

❍ Play Pretzel Pass. Stand or sit in a circle. Give each player a straw or a dowel. Place a pretzel on every other straw or dowel. Encourage the children to pass the pretzel around the circle using only the straws or dowels.

❍ Make Friendship Puzzles. Take photos of the children. Photocopy and enlarge the photos and laminate the copies. Cut the photos into puzzle pieces and invite the children to work the puzzles.

Book Corner

Best Friends by
Steven Kellogg
*Do You Want to Be
My Friend?* by
Eric Carle
*Will You Be My
Friend?* by Nancy
Tafuri
*You Are Special, Little
One* by Nancy
Tafuri

Games

○ Take Hula Hoops® outdoors and encourage the children to play Tug of Peace. It takes cooperative effort. Children sit around the Hula Hoop and grab hold with both hands. *By pulling back on the hoop, can everyone stand up together?*

○ Play I Spy. Gather the children in a group and invite them to name a friend when that child's clothing is described. Choose easy-to-find clothing items at first so children experience a high level of success as they first learn to play. Increase the difficulty as children become more familiar with the game.

○ Make a Find a Friend Game. Take photos of the children. Photocopy two sets of the photos. Glue one set of photos inside a colorful folder in a board game style pathway. Cut the second set of photos out and store them in a zipper-closure bag. Invite the children to match the loose photos to those in the folder.

✓ **English Language Learner Strategy:** Encourage children to match the photos to real children in the classroom. Help them introduce themselves to each friend as rehearsed earlier.

Language

○ Display photos of parents and family members that children may "visit" throughout the day. Also, include items that reflect the cultural experiences of the children to promote a sense of mutual respect and understanding.

Library

○ Encourage the children to read a book with a friend.

Home Connection

○ Suggest that children demonstrate to their families how they introduce one friend to another friend.

The More We Get Together

The more we get together,
Together, together.
The more we get together,
The happier we'll be.

For your friends are my friends
And my friends are your friends.
The more we get together,
The happier we'll be.
(Repeat)

Vocabulary

more
get together
happier
friends

Theme Connections

Cooperation
Friends

Did You Know?

○ There are things that can make the first few weeks of school run more smoothly.
Children, just like adults, need time to adjust to new people and situations. Experience helps to ease transitions but change can still be stressful. Patience and understanding on the part of families, caregivers, and teachers help children learn how to approach new situations with confidence—a skill that helps them make successful transitions throughout their lives.

○ Having appropriate interpersonal skills is essential for enhancing one's social relationships and quality of life. Learning and practicing techniques suitable for children helps them develop and maintain friendships. Friends can improve one's emotional outlook and functioning.

Literacy Links

Oral Language
○ Show the children photos of people working and playing together. Talk about what the people in the photos are doing.
○ Talk about what it means to be a friend. *How do friends treat each other? How do friends show their care and concern for each other? Who is your best friend?*

○ Encourage children to think of things that cannot be done alone, such as playing a baseball game or moving large furniture. Select an activity the children have done as part of a cooperative effort, such as building a fort, decorating their homes for a holiday, and cleaning up after lunch. Ask them to think about how difficult the task might have been if one person had to accomplish it.

○ Teach the children, "For He's a Jolly Good Fellow."

For He's a Jolly Good Fellow
For he's a jolly good fellow,
For he's a jolly good fellow,
For he's a jolly good fellow,
Which nobody can deny.
Which nobody can deny.
Which nobody can deny.
For he's a jolly good fellow,
For he's a jolly good fellow,
For he's a jolly good fellow,
Which nobody can deny.

Curriculum Connections

Art

○ Hang a sheet of butcher paper on the wall. Invite the children to paint a cooperative mural.

Blocks

○ Suggest that the children work together to arrange the blocks end to end to create a bridge that spans the classroom.

Special Needs Adaptation: For children with physical limitations, adapt this activity by attaching a small piece of Velcro to each block. Take a glove or strip of cloth and attach Velcro to it so the child can put on the glove or wrap the cloth around his palm and use it to pick up the blocks. Another adaptation is to provide a small dowel covered in soft material. If the child cannot pick up the block, she can move it into place with her "block moving" stick.

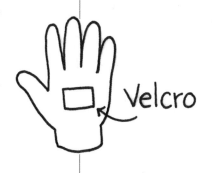

Book Corner

Fine Motor
- Invite children from an older class to come to your classroom and teach the children how to tie their shoes.
- Provide 1″ x 12″ strips of construction paper and glue or paste. Encourage the children to work together to create a chain that will reach from one side of the classroom to the other side of the classroom.

Games
- Play Coin Cover Up. Place about 8″ of water in a plastic tub. Place a quarter in the center of the tub. Give the children each a penny and challenge them to toss their pennies one at a time into the tub in an effort to cover the quarter.

Language
- Provide a 50-piece puzzle. Invite everyone to work on the puzzle over time. Talk with the children as they work the puzzle. *How long would it take one person to finish this puzzle?*

Music and Movement
- Play Cooperative Musical Circles. This game is a variation of Musical Chairs. Make a circle on the floor with masking tape. Play a piece of music. Encourage the children to walk around the circle until the music stops. When the music stops everyone steps into the circle. The idea is to get everyone inside so everyone wins. Continue playing for as long as the children are interested.

Outdoors
- Play Cooperative Hide and Seek. Choose one person to be "IT." IT hides and everyone else tries to find her. Be sure to tell IT that she needs to hide in a place that will accommodate the entire group, because as the children find IT they join her in the hiding place until everyone is hiding together.

Social Studies
- Have the children create art for a sidewalk art sale. Lay the art along the sidewalk and sell it to family members as they pick up their children. Use the profits to purchase something for the classroom or donate it to a good cause.

Home Connection

- Talk with families about participating in a neighborhood co-op, such as a food share or babysitting club.

Say, Say, My Playmate

Vocabulary

apple tree
cellar door
dollies
flu
forevermore
friends
jolly
playmate
rain barrel
rainy day
tearful eyes
tender sighs
three

Theme Connections

Friends
Play

Say, say my playmate,
Come out and play with me.
And bring your dollies three.
Climb up my apple tree.

Look down my rain barrel.
Slide down my cellar door.
And we'll be jolly friends
Forever more.

It was a really rainy day,
And she couldn't come out to play.
With tearful eyes and tender sighs,
I could hear her say:

"I'm sorry, playmate.
I cannot play with you.
My dollies have the flu.
Boo-hoo hoo hoo hoo hoo.

Can't climb your rain barrel.
Can't slide down your cellar door.
But we'll be jolly friends,
Forever more."

Did You Know?

○ Transitioning from home to school can be stressful for children. Friendships can help. Getting on the bus with a favorite playmate or carpooling with a friend can ease the daily transition from home to school. Identifying a buddy at school can also help decrease apprehension about being alone in the new setting (American Academy of Child and Adolescent Psychiatry, 2005).

○ According to Huston and Wright (1996) children spend more time watching television than in any other activity except sleep. They spend significantly less time playing with playmates than they did a decade ago. (Huston, Aletha & J. Wright. 1996. "Television and Socialization of Young Children." Tuning in to Young Viewers: (MacBeth, Tannis, ed.) Sage Publications. University of British Columbia.)

Literacy Links

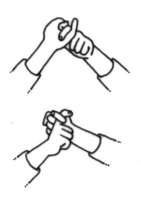

friend

Oral Language

❍ Print *playmate* on chart paper. Draw a line between *play* and *mate*. Point out that playmate is made up of two separate words, *play* and *mate*. Explain that *playmate* is a compound word. Other examples of compound words include *baseball, doghouse,* and *doorbell.*

❍ Teach the children the American Sign Language sign for *friend*.

❍ Talk with the children about how it feels when you want to play with someone and no one is available.

Oral Language/Print Awareness

❍ Discuss how to be kind to a sick friend. Make a list of things you might do; for example, send a card, take her a pot of soup, pick some flowers for her, send her some books to read, draw a picture, and so on.

Print Awareness

❍ Help the children create a list of words used to describe their friends, such as *playmate, buddy, friend, partner, pal, chum,* and *companion.*

Curriculum Connections

Art

❍ Provide paper and markers. Suggest that children design a get-well card for a sick friend.

Discovery

❍ Create a slide by arranging a plank in an inclined position. Give the children blocks and cars to slide down the slide. Which items slide easily and which items are more difficult to slide? Provide sheets of wax paper. *What happens when you slide blocks down the plank on top of sheets of wax paper?*

Dramatic Play

❍ Provide dolls for the children to play with. Provide pretend medicine and other items that the children can use to take care of their "sick" babies.

Fine Motor

○ Show the children how to cut out paper dolls from folded sheets of paper. If necessary, draw a dotted line for the children to use as a cut line.

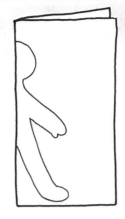 

Language

○ Photocopy the Things I Like to Do Cards (pages 113-114). Color them, cut them out, and laminate them. Have the children arrange the cards from the thing they like to do best with a friend to the thing they like to do least. Younger children can pick the cards that illustrate things they like to do with a friend.

 Special Needs Adaptation: For children with limited vision, enlarge the cards before laminating them so they are easier to see.

Math

○ Print the numeral 3 in the center of a few paper plates. Provide paper dolls. Have the children count three dolls onto each plate.

Science

○ Provide a container to collect rain water. Measure how much rain is collected after a rain. Use the water to water plants.

Snack

○ Serve apple wedges for snack.

Writing

○ Print *playmate* on chart paper. Provide a tray of sand and invite the children to use their finger to copy *playmate* in the sand.

Home Connection

○ Suggest that children talk with their families about who their childhood friends were.

The Kissing Hand by Audrey Penn

Play With Me by Marie Hall Ets

That's What Friends Are For by Valeri Gorbachev

That's What Friends Are For by Florence Parry Heide

That's What Friends Do by Kathryn Cave

Timothy Goes to School by Rosemary Wells

Will I Have a Friend? by Miriam Cohen

Will You Be My Friend? by Nancy Tafuri

SONGS AND ACTIVITIES

Do Your Ears Hang Low?

Do your ears hang low?
Do they wobble to and fro?
Can you tie them in a knot?
Can you tie them in a bow?
Can you throw 'em over your shoulder
Like a Continental soldier?
Do your ears hang low?
(Repeat)

Vocabulary

bow
Continental soldier
ears
hang low
knot
shoulder
throw
tie
to and fro
wobble

Theme Connections

Parts of the Body
Spatial Concepts

Did You Know?

❍ Continental soldiers were soldiers who fought against the British army in the Revolutionary War. Every soldier was issued a musket, bayonet, cartridge box, and tools to keep weapons in working condition. A haversack held important personal belongings as well as eating utensils. Canteens were often suspended from the haversack or worn over the shoulder on a strap.

❍ Some historians believe that the use of the word continental in this song is just a matter of a convenient four-syllable word. The song, which is a popular rugby song, could be written for any type of soldier.

Literacy Links

Oral Language

❍ Talk with the children about what kinds of things they hear. Make a list of all the things that they say they enjoy listening to, such as music, birds singing, water running, and people talking.

❍ Discuss the difference between a knot and a bow. Show examples of each.

❍ Talk about the adjective in the song, *continental*. Make up additional verses to the song using different adjectives to describe a soldier.

❍ Teach the children the American Sign Language signs for *ear, eye, nose,* and *mouth* (pages 115 and 117).

❍ Teach the children "Five Wooden Soldiers" (page 101).

Curriculum Connections

Art

○ Provide a variety of bows, paper, and glue. Encourage the children to make bow collages.

Special Needs Adaptation: Provide bows that have a self-stick surface. This will allow the child to participate without having to tie a bow or use glue. Some children with special needs, especially those with autism spectrum disorder, may be more willing to participate in an activity if they do not have to use glue.

Discovery

○ Provide plastic eggs and playdough. Invite the children to experiment with making the eggs wobble by placing different sizes of balls of playdough inside the eggs. *Do the eggs wobble better when they are heavier or when they are lighter?*

Dramatic Play

○ Cut the crotch out of pairs of clean pantyhose and tie a knot in the legs at the top. Show the children how to put the pantyhose on their heads (waist band around forehead) so they can pretend that they have long ears.

Fine Motor

○ Invite an older classroom of children to come to your classroom and help the children learn to tie bows. Encourage the children to practice tying shoelaces.

Games

○ Talk with the children about how they use their ears for listening. Hide a ticking clock and challenge the children to use their ears to find it.

Gross Motor

○ Fill plastic grocery bags with crumpled paper and tape them together just beneath the handles. Encourage the children to pretend to be Continental soldiers. Show them how to toss the bags over their shoulder (like Santa throws his bag of toys over his shoulder).

○ Invite the children to lie on the floor and draw their arms and legs into their torso to make their body into a ball. Encourage them to wobble by rolling back and forth.

Book Corner

Outdoors

○ Take a listening walk outside. With the children, make a list of things you think you might hear on your walk. Take the list with you. Place a check by the things that you hear. Add things you hear that are not on the list.

Home Connection

○ Suggest that the children use their ears to listen carefully for sounds they hear in their homes, such as clocks ticking, air conditioners or heaters running, electricity coming on, water running, and so on. When they return to school discuss the things they heard.

Head, Shoulders, Knees, and Toes

Vocabulary

ears   mouth
eyes   nose
head   shoulders
knees   toes

Theme Connections

Me
Parts of the Body

Head, shoulders, knees, and toes,
Knees and toes.
Head, shoulders, knees, and toes,
Knees and toes.
Eyes and ears and mouth, and nose,
Head, shoulders, knees, and toes,
Knees and toes.
(Repeat)

Did You Know?

❍ Below is a list of 10 little known but interesting facts about the body. See page 102 for more.

1. More than half the bones in the human body are in the hands and feet.
2. Everyone is colorblind at birth.
3. Food will get to your stomach even if you're standing on your head.
4. It's impossible to sneeze with your eyes open.
5. It takes the interaction of 72 different muscles to produce human speech.
6. Relative to size, the strongest muscle in the body is the tongue.
7. Children grow faster in the springtime.
8. Women blink nearly twice as much as men.
9. There are 10 human body parts that have only three letters (eye, hip, arm, leg, ear, toe, jaw, rib, lip, and gum).
10. Our eyes are the same size from birth, but our nose and ears never stop growing.

Literacy Links

Oral Language

❍ Talk with the children about the safety equipment they should wear when riding a bicycle or skating. Talk about protecting their head, knees, and elbows.

○ Teach children the American Sign Language signs for *head*, *shoulder*, *knee*, and *toe* (pages 116-117)

✓ **English Language Learner Strategy:** On chart paper, print the body parts mentioned in the song in the child's native language. Print the comparable English word beside each word. Place the Head, Shoulder, Knees, and Toes Pattern Cards (page 110) beside each body part. Point to the pictures and then say the words in both languages.

Oral Language/Print Awareness

○ Photocopy the Head, Shoulders, Knees, and Toes Pattern Cards (page 110). Color them, cut them out, and laminate them. Give the cards to a few volunteers and have the volunteers hold up the appropriate card when it is mentioned in the song.

Phonological Awareness

○ Have the children recite and follow the directions in "Say and Touch."

Say and Touch

Say "red," and touch your head.
Say "sky," and touch your eye.
Say "bear," and touch your hair.
Say "hear," and touch your ear.
Say "south," and touch your mouth.
Say "rose," and touch your nose.
Say "in," and touch your chin.
Say "rest," and touch your chest.
Say "farm," and touch your arm.
Say "yummy," and touch your tummy.
Say "bee," and touch your knee.
Say "neat," and touch your feet.

Curriculum Connections

Art

○ Give each child a 9" x 12" sheet of drawing paper. Have the children arrange their papers vertically and then draw large self-portraits (covering the full length of the paper). When they have finished, help them fold their paper into three equal sections. Ask the children questions. *Which parts of your body are in the top section? Which parts are in the middle section? Which parts are in the bottom section?*

ME, MY FAMILY AND FRIENDS

Book Corner

Fine Motor

○ Have the children take off their shoes and then attempt to pick up napkins or scarves with their toes. Can they wave the item they pick up? Can they toss it in the air?

Games

○ Encourage the children to play Simon Says using parts of the body.

Gross Motor

○ Create a maze. Have the children crawl through the maze using their head to push a ball ahead of them.

○ Use masking tape to make a ten-foot long line on the floor. Give the children beanbags. Have them walk the line with the beanbag on their head, then on their shoulder and then on their toes. Can they think of a way to move down the line with a beanbag on their knee?

Language

○ Provide the Head, Shoulders, Knees, and Toes Pattern Cards (page 110). Color them, cut them out, and laminate them. Encourage the children to use the cards to sing the song.

Math

○ Make multiple copies of the Head, Shoulders, Knees, and Toes Pattern Cards (page 110). Don't color them, simply cut them out and laminate them. Have the children make body part patterns by laying the cards out in a pattern, such as head, toes, head, toes, head, toes. Then ask the children to demonstrate the pattern physically.

Music and Movement

○ Teach the children the "A-Root-Chy-Cha" chant (page 99).

Eyes, Nose, Fingers, and Toes by Judy Hindley
From Head to Toe by Eric Carle
Frozen Noses by Jan Carr
Head, Shoulders, Knees and Toes by Annie Kubler
Two Eyes, a Nose and a Mouth by Roberta Intrater

Home Connection

○ Encourage the children to teach their families the song, "Head, Shoulders, Knees, and Toes."

Through the Woods
adapted by Pam Schiller

(Tune: Over the River and Through the Woods)
Over the river and through the woods,
To grandmother's house we go.
The path leads the way to follow and play
Through the dark and scary woods, yes!
Over the river and through the woods,
We're frightened we confess,
But we won't stop. We will not talk,
As along the path we walk.

Vocabulary

along
confess
dark
follow
frightened
grandmother
leads
over
path
play
river
scary
stop
through
woods

Theme Connections

Family
Traditional Tales

Did You Know?

○ The origins of the "Little Red Riding Hood" story can be traced to oral versions that have been around since before the 17th century. In one early Italian example, "La finta nonna" (The False Grandmother), the young girl uses her own cunning to beat the wolf in the end. It has been noted that she does so with no help from any male or older female figure. The woodcutter, added later, limited the girl to a relatively passive role. This has led to criticisms that the story was changed to keep women "in their place," needing the help of a physically superior man such as the woodcutter to save them.

○ In any case, the earliest known printed version is "Le Petit Chaperon Rouge," which has its origins in 17th century French folklore. It was included in the collection *Tales and Stories of the Past with Morals, Tales of Mother Goose* (*Histoires et contes du temps passé, avec des moralités, Contes de ma mère l'Oie*), in 1697 by Charles Perrault.

Literacy Links

Comprehension

○ Read the story of "Little Red Riding Hood." The song is intended to accompany the story.

Oral Language

○ Talk with the children about where their grandparents live. *Who has grandparents that live close by? Who has grandparents that live far away? Do your grandparents live with you?*

○ Talk with the children about things that frighten them. *What frightens you? What do you do when you are afraid?*

Print Awareness

○ Discuss different names that children call their grandparents. Make a list of the many different names for grandparents.

○ Show the children a map. Point out the road that leads from the school to a local park or to the zoo. Show the children the labels on the map.

Curriculum Connections

Art

○ Provide tempera paint, paintbrushes, and paper. Encourage the children to paint the pathway through a "dark and scary" forest.

Blocks

○ Provide props or materials to make props and have the children build a path through the woods. For example, trees can be made from empty toilet paper and paper towel tubes and grass can be made from construction paper or bulletin board paper.

Fine Motor

○ Draw a pathway from one house to another on the bottom of a small box (a stationery box works well). Add trees and bushes to make the path appear to go through the woods. Cut out a small paper doll from drawing paper. Laminate it and glue a magnet to its back. Place the doll by one of the houses on the box bottom. Show the children how to hold a magnet beneath the box and make the doll on the pathway move. Can they move the doll through the woods from one house to the other?

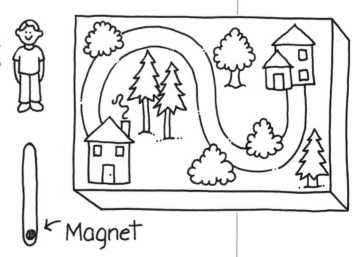

← Magnet

Book Corner

Gross Motor
❍ Use masking tape to make a path on the floor. Place cardboard box houses at both ends of the path. Have the children walk with a basket on their heads from one house to the other along the pathway. Suggest they walk using baby steps on one trip and giant steps on the next. Which type of step gets them to their destination fastest?

Music and Movement
❍ Play scary music with a variety of tempos. Have children tiptoe, run in place, slide, and creep to the music.

Movement/Outdoors
❍ Recite the "Riding Hood Chant" and invite the children to follow the directions.

Riding Hood Chant
Riding Hood, Riding Hood walk so slow.
Riding Hood, Riding Hood tippy, tippy, toe.
Riding Hood, Riding Hood walk, walk, walk.
No! No!, No! Riding Hood do not talk. Shhh!
Shhh, shhh, shhh! Don't make a sound.
Shhh, shhh, shhh! Look all around.
Shhh, shhh, shhh! Tippy-tippy-toe.
Riding Hood, Riding Hood, go, go, go!

Outdoors
❍ Have the children practice the concepts of *over* and *through* by weaving paper streamers in a chain link fence or a plastic laundry basket.

Writing
❍ Print the names that children use for their grandmother on chart paper. Provide magnetic letters and markers and invite the children to copy the names.

Home Connection

❍ Encourage the children to make a phone call to their grandmother or another relative that they have not seen for a while. Suggest that the children tell their grandmother what they did at school that day.

Open, Shut Them

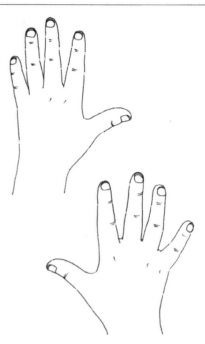

Vocabulary

chin
clap
creep
lap
little
mouth
open
shut
wide

Theme Connections

Opposites
Spatial Concepts

Open, shut them; open, shut them.
Give a little clap, clap, clap.
Open, shut them; open, shut them.
Place them in your lap.

Creep them, creep them,
Creep them, creep them,
Right up to your chin.
Open wide your little mouth,
But do not let them in.

Open, shut them; open, shut them
Give a little clap, clap, clap.
Open, shut them; open, shut them.
Place them in your lap.

Did You Know?

○ Our hands are able to open and close by using a complex combination of muscles, joints, and ligaments.

○ Handedness (the tendency to use one hand rather than the other; for example, left-handed or right-handed) involves more than just the hands. Think about the following tasks. *Which foot do you kick best with? Which ear do you hear most clearly out of? If you want to look at something closely, perhaps using a telescope or a magnifying glass, which eye do you prefer to use?*

○ While many people are all right-sided or all left-sided for these functions, others have a combination of left- and right-dominance. Hand dominance also can vary depending on the task: Some people write using their right hand, but throw, swing a tennis racket, unscrew the lid of a jar, and do virtually everything else left-handed.

○ See page 19 for additional information about hands and fingers.

Literacy Links

Oral Language

○ Ask a volunteer to demonstrate crawling and then creeping. *How are the movements different? What is alike about each movement? Sing the song a second time. This time say crawl instead of creep. What other words could you use?*

○ Read "My Hinges." Invite the children to follow the directions in the text. Discuss the "hinges" in our fingers.

My Hinges

My neck has hinges that move it so.
My shoulders have hinges, just see them go.
My hands and my arms have hinges, too.
My waist will show what hinges can do.
It bends to the front; it bends to the back.
I hope that my hinges never will crack!
My knees have hinges, just see them bend.
My legs have hinges down to the end.
My body has hinges. They do not break.
I use every hinge when I am awake.

Oral Language/Comprehension

○ Have the children search around the room for things that open and shut. Can the children think of something that opens and shuts and is not in the room?

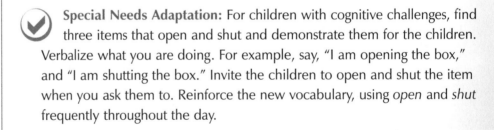

Special Needs Adaptation: For children with cognitive challenges, find three items that open and shut and demonstrate them for the children. Verbalize what you are doing. For example, say, "I am opening the box," and "I am shutting the box." Invite the children to open and shut the item when you ask them to. Reinforce the new vocabulary, using *open* and *shut* frequently throughout the day.

Phonological Awareness

○ Print *clap* and *lap* on chart paper. Help the children understand that the words rhyme. Ask children to brainstorm other words that rhyme with *clap* and *lap*.

Curriculum Connections

Art

○ Provide fingerpaint. Invite the children to fingerpaint. Talk with them about the opening and shutting of their hands as they move the paint around. Encourage the children to make handprints.

Blocks

❍ Invite the children to build a house that has windows and doors that open and close.

Discovery

❍ Give the children a variety of things that open and close, such as a jack-in-the-box, a music box, plastic containers, locks, and lockets. Invite them to sort the items by those that have hinges and those that do not have hinges.

Dramatic Play

❍ Provide a light source. Show the children how to make hand shadow puppets. Challenge children to make hand shadow puppets. *How can you make your puppet talk?*

Fine Motor

❍ Fill a bowl with red and blue stringing beads. Provide tongs. Place a red construction paper wristband on the children's right arm and a blue construction paper wristband on children's left arm. Challenge the children to use the tongs to pick up the red beads with their right hand. Challenge them to use the tongs to pick up the blue beads with their left hand. *Which hand is easier to use?* Discuss hand dominance. Explain that some people are able to use their right hand easier than their left and for some it is the opposite. Discuss the opening and shutting movement of the tongs.

Games

❍ Play Pass the Beanbag. The children sit in a circle. Play music. Have the children pass a beanbag as quickly as possible around the circle. The goal is to not be holding the beanbag when the music stops. Stop the music several times. The child holding the beanbag is caught for a second but can continue to play when the music resumes. Talk with the children about how they must open and close their hands to play this game.

Gross Motor

❍ Make a maze. Have the children navigate the maze first by crawling and then by creeping. *Which is easier?*

Book Corner

Language

❍ Teach the children the two fingerplays below.

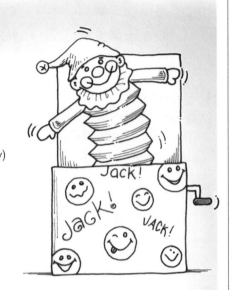

Jack-in-the-Box

Jack-in-the-box (tuck thumb into fist)
Oh, so still.
Won't you come out? (raise hand slightly)
Yes, I will. (pop thumb out of fist)

Wake Up, Jack!

Jack-in-the-box, jack-in-the-box,
Wake up, wake up, somebody knocks.
One time, two times, three times, four.
Jack pops out of his little round door.

Outdoors

❍ Provide a small ball. Have the children attempt to catch and throw the ball without opening and closing their hands. Is anyone successful?

Snack

❍ Discuss how the mouth moves when eating. *What allows the mouth to open and close?* Have the children place their hands on their jaws and feel the movement of their jaw.

Writing

❍ Trace around magnetic letters to print *open* on sheets of drawing paper. Provide magnetic letters and invite the children to place the letters over the letters you have traced. Remind the children that they may see *open* signs in windows of stores when the stores are open for business.

Home Connection

❍ Encourage the children to survey their home for things that open and shut. Discuss what they find when they return to school.

Today Is a Birthday

Vocabulary

birthday
congratulate
dreams
friend
goodness
Happy Birthday
know
laughing
smiling
somebody
today
whom
wishes
wonder

Theme Connections

Celebrations
Friends

Today is a birthday.
I wonder for whom.
We know it's for somebody
Right in this room.
So look all around you
For somebody who
Is laughing and smiling.
My goodness, it's you!

Happy birthday, my friend,
   (or child's name)
From all of us to you.
Happy birthday, good friend,
Happy birthday to you.
We congratulate you,
With all good wishes for you.
Happy birthday, dear friend,
May all of your good dreams come true!

Did You Know?

- On birthdays in Denmark, people hang a birthday flag in the window. For children's birthdays, the presents are placed around the child's bed while he or she is sleeping, so the child will see the presents upon awakening!
- In Ireland, the birthday child is lifted by the hands and feet, and "bumped" on the floor for good luck. The number of bumps given is the age of the child, plus one for luck!
- All Japanese children used to celebrate their birthdays on January 1st, regardless of when they were born. Today, most Japanese children celebrate on their actual birthdays.
- On a child's first birthday in Korea, the birthday child is dressed in special clothes. The friends and family all visit for a big feast and bring money, food, and gifts for the child. All the gifts are placed in front of the child, and the child's future is foretold by the items he or she picks up.
- In Mexico, families use papier-mâché to make a piñata in the shape of an animal. They fill it with sweets or other treats and then hang it from the ceiling by a rope. They blindfold the birthday child and then he or she hits

the piñata with a stick until it cracks open and the contents spill out. All the treats are shared.

○ Instead of a birthday cake, many Russian children are given a birthday pie! A birthday message is carved into the pie crust.

Literacy Links

Oral Language

○ Teach the children the American Sign Language sign for *Happy Birthday* (page 116).

○ Talk with the children about birthdays. *How do you celebrate birthdays? How many have you had?*

○ Say the following fingerplay, and have the children perform the hand motions.

Birthday Candles
Birthday candles one, two, three! (hold up one finger for each number counted)
Birthday candles, just for me! (point to self)
Last year three, next year four, (hold up three fingers on left hand and four fingers on right)
Birthday candles, I want more! (hold up 10 fingers)

Curriculum Connections

Art

○ Encourage the children to design birthday cards for a friend or family member.

Cooking

○ Encourage the children to follow the Baggie Ice Cream Recipe (page 103) to create a birthday snack.

Dramatic Play

○ Provide birthday props such as hats, streamers, candles, and birthday cards. Invite the children to have a pretend birthday party.

Fine Motor

○ Provide small boxes, tape, bows, and wrapping paper. Challenge the children to pretend to wrap birthday presents.

Book Corner

A Chair for My Mother by Vera B. Williams
Flower Garden by Eve Bunting
Happy Birthday to You! by Dr. Seuss
Moira's Birthday by Robert Munsch
Not Yet, Yvette by Helen Ketteman

Games

○ Invite the children to play Drop the Clothespin in the Bottle. Place a wide-mouth plastic bottle on the floor and provide clothespins. Challenge the children to stand over the bottle and drop clothespins from waist high with a goal of getting as many clothespins as possible into the bottle.

Language

○ Cut out chocolate, vanilla, and strawberry cakes from brown, white, and pink felt. Cut out a variety of colorful icings and candles from different colors of felt. Encourage the children to make felt birthday cakes on the flannel board.

Math

○ Provide playdough, a rolling pin, and birthday candles. Have the children roll out five playdough birthday cakes. Encourage the children to place one birthday candle on the first cake, two on the second, three on the third, and so on. Suggest that they say the rhyme, "Birthday Candles" while they work.

○ Make a graph of the children's ages. Discuss *less* and *more* and the *same* as they apply to the information on the graph.

Writing

○ Print *Happy Birthday* on large index cards. Give the children a squirt bottle of colored glue to represent cake icing. Invite them to trace over the letters with the colored glue.

Home Connection

○ Encourage the children to ask their families to share their memories of childhood birthdays.

My Mother Is a Baker

(Tune: Johnny Works With One Hammer)
My mother is a baker,
A baker, a baker.
My mother is a baker.
She always goes like this:
Yum, yum!

My father is a trash man,
A trash man, a trash man.
My father is a trash man.
He always goes like this:
Yum, yum!
Pee-eww!

My sister is a singer… Yum, yum! Pee-eww! Laa dee da!
My doggy is a kisser… Yum, yum! Pee-eww! Laa dee da! Slurp, slurp!
My kitty is a scratcher… Yum, yum! Pee-eww! Laa dee da! Slurp,
    slurp! Scratch, scratch!
My baby is a whiner… Yum, yum! Pee-eww! Laa dee da! Slurp, slurp!
    Scratch, scratch! Whaa, whaa!
My grandpa is an engineer… Yum, yum! Pee-eww! Laa dee da! Slurp,
    slurp! Scratch, scratch! Whaa, whaa! Toot, toot!
My grandma is a tickler… Yum, yum! Pee-eww! Laa dee da! Slurp,
    slurp! Scratch, scratch! Whaa, whaa! Toot, toot! Ha, ha, ha!
My brother is a cowboy… Yum, yum! Pee-eww! Laa dee da! Scratch,
    scratch! Whaa, whaa! Toot, toot! Ha, ha, ha! Yahoo!

Vocabulary

baby
baker
brother
cowboy
doggy
engineer
father
grandma
grandpa
kisser
kitty
mother
scratcher
singer
sister
tickler
trash man
whiner

Theme Connections

Family
Workers

Did You Know?

- The first observance of Labor Day is believed to have been a parade on September 5, 1882, in New York City, probably organized by Peter J. McGuire, a Carpenters and Joiners Union secretary. By 1893, more than half the states were observing a "Labor Day" on one day or another.
- The law establishing Labor Day as a federal holiday was passed by Congress in 1894. President Grover Cleveland signed the bill, designating the first Monday in September as Labor Day.
- Americans work in a wide variety of occupations. According to the latest census, the ten most common occupations are secretaries and administrative assistants; retail salespersons; driver/sales workers and truck drivers; elementary and middle school teachers; cashiers; supervisors/managers of retail sales workers; registered nurses; customer

service representatives; janitors and building cleaners; laborers and freight, stock, and material movers.
Source: U.S. Census Bureau, Public Information Office

Literacy Links

Letter Recognition
○ Print *yum-yum* on chart paper. Ask the children to identify the letters in each word. Write some of the other sound words in the song on chart paper and ask the children to identify the letters.

Oral Language
○ Encourage children to talk about their families, including jobs that their family members perform.

English Language Learner Strategy: Ask family members to make posters for their family. Suggest that they draw a family portrait or use a photograph of the family or family members. They might also add something about things the family enjoys doing together like planting a garden, camping, going to the movies or traveling. Encourage families to add anything to their poster that helps describe their family. Each poster will be unique. Ask the children to use the posters to talk about their family. Choose items on the poster and ask the children to name and describe the item. Assist when needed. Hang the posters in the classroom.

Phonological Awareness
○ Discuss the sounds in the song. Are any of them *onomatopoeic* words (words that sound like the sound they are describing)? Discuss nonsense sounds.

Curriculum Connections

Discovery
○ Provide feathers, a straw, a cotton swab, and a pipe cleaner. Have the children try brushing each item over the skin on the underside of their arm. *Which item would make the best "tickler" for Grandmother?*

Book Corner

Cowboy Small by
Lois Lenski
*"Fire! Fire!" Said
Mrs. McGuire* by
Bill Martin, Jr.
Guess Who? by
Margaret Miller

Dramatic Play

❍ Provide props for a bakery, such as aprons, pans, rolling pins, playdough, and a cash register. Invite the children to pretend they are running a bakery.

❍ Provide baby dolls and have the children care for them. How do they keep the babies from crying?

Field Trip

❍ Visit a bakery. Is there a baker in one of the children's families?

Games

❍ Invite the children to play Tummy Ticklers. Have children lie on the floor on their backs with their heads on someone else's tummy. Do something silly to make the children start laughing. *What is making your heads jiggle?* This activity should cause contagious laughing

Music

❍ Provide play microphones or pretend microphones (empty toilet paper tubes work well), a tape recorder, and rhythm band instrument. Invite the children to pretend they are singers in a recording studio making a recording.

Outdoors

❍ Give the children litter bags and encourage them to be trash collectors. Have them pick up the playground trash. **Safety Note**: Provide sturdy work gloves and/or disposal gloves to protect the children's hands.

❍ Provide pie tins, twigs, leaves, and mud. Invite the children to be bakers baking mud pies.

Home Connection

❍ Suggest that children ask their family members about their jobs and jobs they might like to do.

Lavender's Blue

Vocabulary

blue	king
corn	lavender
fork	plough
friends	queen
green	thresh
hay	whilst
heart	work

Theme Connections

Colors
Friends
Make-Believe

Lavender's blue, dilly, dilly,
Lavender's green.
When you are King, dilly, dilly,
I shall be Queen.

Who told you so, dilly, dilly,
Who told you so?
'Twas my own heart, dilly, dilly,
That told me so.

Call up your friends, dilly, dilly,
Set them to work.
Some to the plough, dilly, dilly,
Some to the fork.

Some to the hay, dilly, dilly,
Some to thresh corn.
Whilst you and I, dilly, dilly,
Keep ourselves warm.

Lavender's blue, dilly, dilly,
Lavender's green.
When you are King, dilly, dilly,
I shall be Queen.

Who told you so, dilly, dilly,
Who told you so?
'Twas my own heart, dilly, dilly,
That told me so.
'Twas my own heart, dilly, dilly,
That told me so.

Did You Know?

○ "Lavender's Blue" was written in England in 1665.

○ English and Irish love ballads from the 1600's include "Scarborough Fair," "Black Is the Color of My True Love's Hair," "The Water Is Wide," "Greensleeves," and "She Moved Through the Fair." Folk songs from this time period often told of unrequited love and have remained popular over the centuries. You can hear echoes of them today in such hits as "My Heart Will Go On" and "The First Time Ever I Saw Your Face."

○ The original song was called "The Kind Country Lovers" and was first printed in 1685. It had a number of verses and was probably part of a festival in which a king and queen were chosen from the village youth. The original lyrics are:

Lavender's blue, diddle diddle
Lavender's green,
When I am king, diddle diddle
You shall be queen.
Lavender's green, diddle diddle
Lavender's blue,
You must love me, diddle diddle
'Cause I love you.

Literacy Links

Letter Knowledge

❍ Print *dilly dilly* on chart paper. Ask the children to identify the letters. *Which letter appears more than once in each word?* Print *diddle diddle* beneath *dilly dilly*. Explain that when the song was first written, long ago, *diddle* was used instead of *dilly*. Discuss the letters in *diddle*. *Which letter appears more than once?* Sing the song, substituting *diddle* for *dilly*. Which version do the children like best?

Oral Language

❍ Talk about the color lavender. *What things are lavender? Is anyone wearing lavender color clothing? Is there anything in the room that is lavender?* Sing "The Iguana in Lavender Socks" (page 98).

❍ Discuss kings and queens. *Do they still exist? Where do they live? Where do they live in fairy tales? What do they wear? What do they do?* Show the children pictures in books of real and pretend kings and queens.

Phonological Awareness

❍ Ask the children to think of words that rhyme with *blue*. Ask them to think of words that rhyme with *green*. Challenge them to think of words that rhyme with *lavender* (nonsense words are fine).

❍ Encourage the children to help identify the rhyming word pairs in the song, such as *green/Queen*.

Curriculum Connections

Art

❍ Provide paper, paintbrushes, and lavender paint for the children to use for their easel paintings.

❍ Invite the children to make lavender collages with a variety of lavender papers, bows, and beads.

Construction

❍ Provide tagboard and a pattern of a crown for children to trace. Have the children trace and cut out the crown. Provide glue, glitter, confetti, and jewels for the children to use to decorate their crowns.

Dramatic Play

○ Provide royal props, caps, scepters, and crowns. Invite the children to pretend to be kings and queens.

Fine Motor

○ Provide corn on the cob. Show the children how to shuck the corn. After it is shucked, cook it and serve it for lunch or snack. **Note:** Make sure children wash their hands before shucking the corn.

Games

○ Play Drop the Lavender Handkerchief. The children form a circle. Select one child to be "IT." IT walks around the circle and eventually drops the handkerchief behind another child. The selected child chases IT around the circle and attempts to tag him before he can get back around to the child's place in the circle.

Language

○ Cut large hearts from lavender construction paper. Laminate them and cut them into puzzle pieces. Invite the children to work the puzzles. Talk with the children as they work the puzzles. Discuss the way the pieces go together.

Math

○ Away from the children, use gold spray paint to make gold coins (adult-only step). Print numerals one through ten on small paper bags. Have the children pretend to be kings and queens counting their gold by placing the same number of coins in the bag as indicated by the numeral on the outside of the bag.

Snack

○ Mix red and blue food coloring with cream cheese to make a lavender spread. Help the children use heart-shaped cookie cutters to cut a heart from a slice of bread and then spread it with lavender cream cheese.

Home Connection

○ Have the children search at home for something that is lavender. Encourage them to bring the item to school. Create a display of lavender things.

The Iguana in Lavender Socks by Pam Schiller

Lavender Finds a Friend by Cicely Mary Barker

The Lavender Llama by Tandy Braid

Lavender's Blue by Kathleen Lines

Cap, Mittens, Shoes, and Socks

(Tune: Head, Shoulder, Knees and Toes)
Cap, mittens, shoes and socks.
Shoes and socks!
Cap, mittens, shoes and socks
Shoes and socks!
Pants and belt, and shirt and tie
Go together wet or dry,
Wet or dry!
(Repeat)

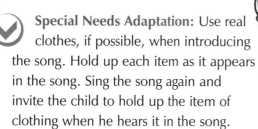 **Special Needs Adaptation:** Use real clothes, if possible, when introducing the song. Hold up each item as it appears in the song. Sing the song again and invite the child to hold up the item of clothing when he hears it in the song.

Vocabulary

belt
cap
dry
hat
mittens
pants
shirt
shoes
socks
tie
wet

Theme Connections

Clothing
Me

Did You Know?

❍ "Jeans" as we know them today were invented in 1873 by Jacob Davis due to meet the need of miners and other working-class men for durable, stronger clothing.

❍ Flappers were the first women in the 1920s to rebel against traditional clothing standards. They rejected drab Victorian clothes and began expressing their desire to break free of traditional conventions through their clothing.

❍ Some Americans, out of respect for their religion and/or culture, wear traditional clothing; for example, some Muslim women wear burkas and some Indian women wear saris.

❍ Most early childhood experts agree that by age two and a half, children should begin to dress and undress themselves including buttoning easy-to-button buttons. By age four, nine out of ten children are able to button the buttons on their clothing.

Literacy Links

Oral Language

❍ Help the children add verses to the song using different clothing items.

❍ Teach the American Sign Language signs for *cap (hat)* and *mittens* (pages 116-117).

❍ Talk with the children about different types of clothing. *How is winter clothing different from summer clothing? How is rain gear different from regular clothes?*

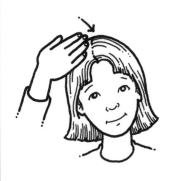

cap/hat

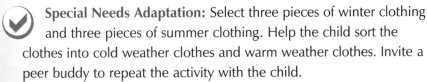 **Special Needs Adaptation:** Select three pieces of winter clothing and three pieces of summer clothing. Help the child sort the clothes into cold weather clothes and warm weather clothes. Invite a peer buddy to repeat the activity with the child.

❍ Discuss getting dressed. *Can you dress by yourself? Who helps you get dressed?* Share the poem, "I Can Do It Myself" with the children.

I Can Do It Myself
Hat on head, just like this
Pull it down, you see.
I can put my hat on
All by myself, just me.

One arm in, two arms in,
Buttons, one, two, three.
I can put my coat on
All by myself, just me.

Toes in first, heels down next,
Pull and pull, then see—
I can put my boots on
All by myself, just me.

Fingers here, thumbs right here,
Hands warm as can be.
I can put my mittens on
All by myself, just me.

Phonological Awareness

❍ Say *rock, clock, cat,* and *lock.* Ask the children to tell you the word that does not rhyme with *sock.*

Print Awareness

❍ Print the song on chart paper. Move your hand beneath the words as you sing the song. Point out the left-to-right and top-to-bottom progression of the words. Sing the song reversing the clothing items. What happens?

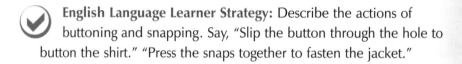

English Language Learner Strategy: Show the children photos of each clothing item or real clothing items prior to singing the song. Use the photos or items as props as you sing the song. Lay the photos or items on the floor. Sing the song a second time. This time have the children point to the item as it is mentioned.

Curriculum Connections

Dramatic Play

❍ Provide dress-up clothes, particularly those mentioned in the song. Invite the children to play dress up.

Fine Motor

❍ Provide a variety of clothing items that snap or button. Encourage the children to practice buttoning and snapping the clothing items.

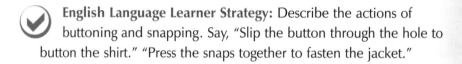

English Language Learner Strategy: Describe the actions of buttoning and snapping. Say, "Slip the button through the hole to button the shirt." "Press the snaps together to fasten the jacket."

Math

❍ Provide a basket of mittens and socks. Ask the children to pair the mittens and the socks.

❍ Provide a variety of belts. Have the children arrange the belts from the longest to the shortest.

Music and Movement

❍ Have the children remove their shoes and dance in their socks.

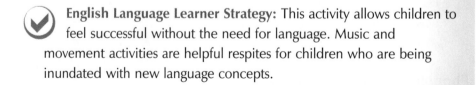

English Language Learner Strategy: This activity allows children to feel successful without the need for language. Music and movement activities are helpful respites for children who are being inundated with new language concepts.

Outdoors

❍ Provide socks, a tub of soapy water, a tub of clear water, and a drying rack or clothesline. Invite the children to wash the socks and hang them to dry.

CAP, MITTENS, SHOES, AND SOCKS

Book Corner

Caps, Hats, Socks, and Mittens by Louise W. Borden
Whose Hat? by Margaret Miller

Snack

○ Serve cookies and juice. Ask the children to say which food item is wet and which one is dry.

Writing

○ Print the song on chart paper and place it in the writing center. Provide markers and paper. Encourage the children to copy words in the song.

Home Connection

○ Challenge the children to find one item mentioned in the song in their home or closet.

SONGS AND ACTIVITIES

71

Here We Go 'Round the Mulberry Bush

Here we go 'round the mulberry bush,
The mulberry bush, the mulberry bush.
Here we go 'round the mulberry bush,
So early in the morning.

This is the way we wash our clothes,
Wash our clothes, wash our clothes.
This is the way we wash our clothes,
So early in the morning.

Additional verses:
This is the way we take out the trash…
This is the way we sweep the house…
This is the way we mow the yard…

Here we go 'round the mulberry bush,
The mulberry bush, the mulberry bush.
Here we go 'round the mulberry bush,
So early in the morning.

Vocabulary

clothes
early
morning
mow
mulberry bush
'round
sweep
trash
wash

Theme Connections

Days of the Week
Work

Did You Know?

❍ "Here We Go 'Round the Mulberry Bush" is an English nursery rhyme.

❍ When Britain tried to grow its own silk, they planted mulberry trees, which are a food source for silkworms, all over, including in prison yards. The idea was that the prisoners would produce silk. The term "to go 'round the mulberry bush" became a euphemism for being in prison.

> Source: Roberts, Chris. *Heavy words lightly thrown: The reason behind the rhyme*. Granta Publications, 2004

❍ The white mulberry tree was introduced into America in early colonial times and naturalized and hybridized with the native red mulberry. The red or American mulberry is native to eastern United States from Massachusetts to Kansas and down to the Gulf coast.

❍ There are many famous mulberry trees in England. Those of Syon House, Brentford are of special historical interest and include what is reported to be the oldest tree of its kind in England, reportedly introduced from Persia in 1548.

Literacy Links

Oral Language
○ Talk with the children about household chores. *Who helps with chores at your house? Who cuts the grass? Who washes the clothes?* Discuss classroom chores. *Who keeps the toys picked up? Are chores easier when everyone helps?*

✓ **Special Needs Adaptation:** Cut out pictures from magazines of people doing household chores and show them to the child. Start with two pictures and ask the child to tell you what the person in the picture is doing.

Oral Language/Print Awareness
○ Challenge the children to add verses to the song. Print their new verses on chart paper. Move your hand beneath the words as you sing the song.

Print Awareness/Letter Knowledge
○ Sing the original version of the song (page 97). Print each of the days of the week on chart paper. *What is interesting about the last three letters in each word?* Identify the other letters in each day. *Which days start with the same letter?*

Curriculum Connections

Art
○ Invite the children to use paper, paintbrushes, and green and brown tempera paint to paint a mulberry bush.

Discovery
○ Explain to the children that silkworms attach to mulberry bushes and that people like to grow the trees so that they can get the silk produced by the silkworm. Provide photos of silkworms and some silk items, such as scarves, ties, blouses, and slips for the children to explore.

Dramatic Play
○ Provide doll clothing, soapy water, rinse water, and a drying rack. Invite the children to wash the doll clothes.

Book Corner

Here We Go Round the Mulberry Bush by Pam Adams

Here We Go 'Round the Mulberry Bush by Will Hillenbrand

The Very Hungry Caterpillar by Eric Carle

Fine Motor
❍ Provide a hand broom and dustpan. Spill a small quantity of pebbles on the floor. Invite the children to sweep the pebbles into the dustpan.

Language
❍ Invite the children to look through magazines for people doing household chores. Encourage them to cut the photos out of the magazines and make chore collages. Talk to the children about what is happening in the photos.

Music and Movement
❍ Dance the Here We Go 'Round the Mulberry dance. Have the children hold hands and walk in a circle. Stop for each verse and act out the activity the verse describes.
❍ Provide silk scarves and encourage the children to dance creatively with the scarves to classical music.

Snack
❍ Serve crackers and mulberry jam for snack.

Writing
❍ List the days of the week on chart paper. Provide magnetic letters and invite the children to copy the days.

Home Connection

❍ Have the children discuss household chores with their families. Do they have special days for cutting grass or washing clothes?

The Farmer in the Dell

Vocabulary

alone	farmer
cat	mouse
cheese	nurse
child	wife
dell	

Theme Connections

Family

Farms

The farmer in the dell,
The farmer in the dell,
Hi-ho the derry-o,
The farmer's in the dell.

The farmer takes a wife.
The farmer takes a wife.
Hi-ho the derry-o,
The farmer takes a wife.

Other verses:
The wife takes a child…
The child takes a nurse…
The nurse takes a cat…
The cat takes a mouse…
The mouse takes the cheese…

The cheese stands alone.
The cheese stands alone.
Hi-ho the derry-o,
The cheese stands alone!

Did You Know?

○ In 2004, less than 1% of the 285,000,000 people living in the United States claimed farming as an occupation (and about 2% actually live on farms).

○ In 2004, there were 2,113,470 farmers in the United States. The average farm was 443 acres. Only 106,045 of these farms are dairy farms
Source: U.S. Department of Agriculture www.usda.gov

○ Dairy farm facts: full-grown Holstein Cows can weigh as much as 1,400 pounds; dairy cows drink the equivalent of a bathtub full of water and eat about 40 pounds of feed and hay and 50 pounds of silage (a mixture of corn and grass that is stored in silos) every day; and it takes about 20 minutes to milk a cow.

Literacy Links

Comprehension/Print Awareness

○ Sing the song substituting characters from a favorite story. For example:

The Little Red Hen characters,
The Little Red Hen characters,
Hi-ho the derry-o,
The Little Red Hen characters.

Little Red Hen chooses a dog…
Dog chooses a cat…

Print their new verses on chart paper and move your hands under the words as you sing the new song.

Phonological Awareness

❍ Sing "ti-to the tarry-o" in place of "hi-ho the derry-o." Can the children hear the differences in the words? Try other consonant substitutions, such as "bi-bo the berry-o" and "si-so the serry-o."

Curriculum Connections

Blocks

❍ In the block area, add farm props, such as plastic animals, round boxes for a silo, and brown and green fabric for the ground. Encourage the children to build a farm.

> ✓ **Special Needs Adaptation:** Explain each prop to the children with special needs. Find a peer buddy to help the child as he builds his farm. If the child is hesitant to participate in the activity, model for him how he might build a farm. Often, children with special needs want to participate in classroom activities, but they don't know how to participate.

Cooking

❍ Invite the children to follow the rebus directions for Making Butter (page 107) to make their own jar of butter. Provide crackers for them to taste their butter.

Dramatic Play

❍ Fill the center with farmer clothes, such as overalls, hats, boots, and bandanas. Encourage the children to pretend that they working on a farm.

Field Trip

❍ Visit a farm or ask a farmer to visit the classroom.

Math/Fine Motor

❍ Cut small holes in the top of margarine container lids. Print the numerals 1-5 on the lids, one number per lid. Provide popcorn kernels and tweezers. Have the children use the tweezers to place the number of corn kernels into the margarine tub that is indicated

Tweezers ↑   Popcorn ↙

by the numeral on the container's lid. Pop the popcorn for snack after children are finished counting kernels.

Movement

❍ Select one child to pantomime the actions of a farm animal. The remaining children guess which animal the first child is mimicking. Make sure all the children get a turn to do this.

Music

❍ Invite the children to sing barnyard songs, such as "Bingo," "Old MacDonald Had a Farm," and "Six White Ducks."

❍ Teach the children the song, "We're on the Way to Grandpa's Farm."

We're on the Way to Grandpa's Farm
Chorus:
We're on our way,
We're on our way,
We're on our way to Grandpa's farm.
We're on our way,
We're on our way,
We're on our way to Grandpa's farm.

Down on Grandpa's farm there is a big brown cow.
Down on Grandpa's farm there is a big brown cow.

(Chorus)

The cow, it goes a lot like this... (moo)
The cow, it goes a lot like this... (moo)

(Chorus)

The chicken, it goes a lot like this... (cluck, cluck)
The chicken, it goes a lot like this... (cluck, cluck)

(Chorus)

The horse, it goes a lot like this... (neigh, neigh)
The horse, it goes a lot like this... (neigh, neigh)

(Chorus)

The banjo, it goes a lot like this...
The banjo, it goes a lot like this...

Book Corner

Annabel by Janice Boland

Barnyard Banter by Denise Fleming

Barnyard Song by Rhonda Gowler Greene

Big Red Barn by Margaret Wise Brown

Early Morning in the Barn by Nancy Tafuri

The Farmer in the Dell by Pam Adams

The Little Red Hen by Paul Galdone

Old MacDonald Had a Farm by Pam Adams

Spots, Feathers, and Curly Tails by Nancy Tafuri

Who Took the Farmer's Hat? by Joan L. Nodset

Science
○ Plant a small vegetable garden on the playground or plant seeds in cups and place them in an inside window.

Home Connection

○ Suggest that families talk with their children about products that come from farms when they visit the grocery store.

I Have Something in My Pocket

Vocabulary

across   happy
belongs   long while
convenient   place
face   pocket
guess   smile

Theme Connections

Expressions   Humor

I have something in my pocket
It belongs across my face.
I keep it very close at hand
In a most convenient place.
I bet you couldn't guess it
If you guessed a long, long while.
So I'll take it out and I'll put it on.
It's a great big happy SMILE!

Did You Know?

○ A smile is a universal expression of happiness recognized as such by all cultures.
○ A smile is the most frequently used facial expression. It takes as few as five pairs of facial muscles and as many as all 53 to smile. Regardless of the precise number of muscles used, smiling causes far fewer muscles to contract and expand than frowning.
○ Smiling releases endorphins and makes us feel better. Even faking a smile can make you feel happier.
○ People are born with the ability to smile. (They don't copy the expression; babies who are born blind smile.)
○ A newborn shows a preference for a smiling face over a non-smiling face.
○ Women smile more than men.
○ There are 18 different kinds of smiles used in a variety of social situations.
○ Human beings can differentiate between a smile of joy and happiness and a social smile. It's in the eyes (literally)!
○ A smiling person is judged to be more pleasant, attractive, sincere, sociable, and competent than a non-smiling person.

Literacy Links

Oral Language

○ Ask each child to smile while looking into a small mirror. Ask each child to describe his face when he is smiling.
○ Teach the children the American Sign Language sign for *smile* (page 117).

Oral Language/Listening

❍ Talk with the children about smiling. *What makes you smile? How do you feel when people smile at you? When someone smiles at you, what do you think they are saying? Are smiles contagious?* Read the listening story "What Makes Me Laugh?" (page 102). Encourage the children to add things to the story.

Oral Language/Segmentation

❍ Clap the syllables in *happy*. Sing the song again substituting another two-syllable word for happy.

Phonological Awareness

❍ Talk with the children about how rhyming words are words that have the same ending sound. Ask questions. *Which word does not rhyme with smile: while, tile, mile, song, or file? What words rhyme with face or hand?*

Curriculum Connections

Art

❍ Provide tempera paint and invite the children to paint a smiling face.
❍ Place fingerpaint directly on a table top. Invite the children to make happy faces in the paint.

Fine Motor

❍ Ask the children to look through magazines, cut out pictures of people smiling, and glue the pictures onto paper to create a collage of smiles.
❍ Suggest that the children use playdough to create smiling faces.

Games

❍ Make two photocopies of the Happy Face Match-Up Patterns (page 109). Color them and cut them out. Give the children the cards and suggest they play Happy Face Concentration.
❍ Make two photocopies of the Happy Face Match-Up Patterns (page 109). Color them and cut them out. Spread one set of cards on the floor. Use the second set of cards as drawing cards. Use masking tape to make a throw line. Have the children draw a card and then toss a beanbag to land on the face that matches the face they drew.

> **English Language Learner Strategy**
> Review the game rules. Stress key game vocabulary, such as *match*, *toss*, and *your turn*.

Language

○ Decorate a 9″ x 12″ manila envelope to look like a pocket. Cut four or five windows in one side of the envelope (cut three sides of a square, leaving one side as the hinge of the window). Place a photograph inside the pocket and then have the children open the windows one at a time until they have enough clues to identify what who or what is in the photo.

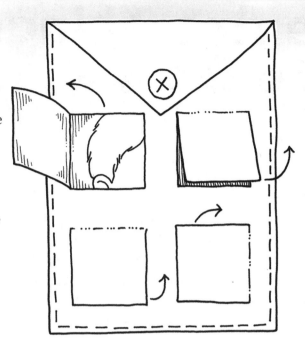

○ Cut a pocket from a large pair of jeans or make a pocket using scraps of fabric. Place an item in the pocket and encourage the children to put their hand in the pocket and describe what they feel. Can they guess what is in the pocket?

✓ **Special Needs Adaptation:** For a child with cognitive challenges, adapt this activity by showing the child three items, such as a ball, small block, and small toy car. Place the items behind you, where the child can't see which one you are putting in the pocket. It will be easier for the child to guess what is in the pocket if he has already seen the item. This gives him fewer choices and still allows him to fully participate in the fun.

Writing

○ Print *smile* on chart paper. Encourage the children to use Scrabble letters, felt letters, and magnetic letters to copy the word.

Home Connection

○ Encourage the children to see if smiling is contagious. Have them smile at their family members to see if their family members smile back.

Don't Make Me Laugh by James Stevenson
Giggle Belly by Page Sakelaris
Giggle, Giggle, Quack by Doreen Cronin
If You're Happy and You Know It! by Jan Ormerod
Katy No-Pockets by Emmy Payne
One Smile by Cindy McKinley
Smile a Lot! by Nancy L. Carlson
Toes Have Wiggles, Kids Have Giggles by Harriet Ziefert

SONGS AND ACTIVITIES

These Are Things I Like to Do by Pam Schiller

(Tune: London Bridge Is Falling Down)
These are things I like to do,
Like to do, like to do.
These are things I like to do.
I know a trick or two.

This is the way I read a book,
Read a book, read a book.
This is the way I read a book.
I know a trick or two.

Additional verses:
This is the way I paint a picture…
This is the way I throw the ball…
This is the way I ride my bike…
This is the way I climb a tree…
This is the way I help my dad…
This is the way we sing our song,
Sing our song, sing our song.

This is the way we sing our song.
We've sung our song, now how
'bout you?

Special Needs Adaptation: For children with cognitive challenges, teach just two verses of the song, such as "read a book" and "throw a ball." Encourage the children to act out the activity while you sing the song. It is often easier for a child with special needs to participate if the activity involves something that is concrete and familiar to them.

Vocabulary

ball	read
bike	ride
book	sing
climb	song
dad	things
help	throw
like	tree
paint	trick
picture	two

Theme Connections

Me
Things I Like to Do

Did You Know?

❍ When asked what they enjoy doing, some of things children say include:
  ○ Play outside
  ○ Play with playdough
  ○ Build with blocks
  ○ Dance
  ○ Make personal pizzas
  ○ Glue anything to paper (glitter, scraps of paper, leaves)
  ○ String and unstring beads
  ○ Make-believe with things from home (straws, crackers, clean plastic bottles, curlers)

Literacy Links

Oral Language

○ Talk with the children about playing with friends and playing alone. Which do the children prefer?

○ Encourage the children to think about their favorite school activity. Make a list of their favorite activities.

○ Talk about things that the children like to do on the playground. Encourage the children to act out "Fun at the Playground."

Fun at the Playground
Climb on the ladder and down we slide,
Then on the teeter totter we ride.
Swinging, swinging, way up high,
Stretching, stretching to touch the sky.
Around we go on the merry-go-round,
Having fun on the playground.

Print Awareness

○ Encourage the children to brainstorm a list of things they like to do. Add verses to the song using the list of things the children have generated.

Curriculum Connections

Art

○ Provide paper, paintbrushes, and tempera paint. Invite the children to paint a picture of something they like to do.

○ Encourage the children to use markers, crayons, and paper to draw their favorite toy.

Games

○ Teach the children how to play Tic Tac Toe. Encourage them to play a game of two with a friend.

✓ **English Language Learner Strategy:** Pair a child who is learning to speak English with a child who has well-developed expressive language skills. If possible, repeat the direction in both languages. Review the meaning of spatial concepts (*in the box, below, beside*) before starting the game.

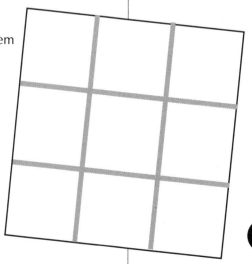

Book Corner

Eppie M Says by
    Dunrae
Things I Like by
    Anthony Browne
Things I Like to Do
    by Leon
    Archibald
Things I Like to Do
    by Beth Clure

Language
○ Photocopy the Things I Like to Do Cards (pages 113-114). Color them, cut them out, and laminate them. Invite the children to look at each card and decide if it is something they like to do. Challenge them to arrange the cards from the thing they enjoy most to the thing they enjoy the least.

Library
○ Suggest that the children invite a friend to read a book together.

Outdoors
○ Take balls outdoors and encourage the children to throw the balls to one another.
○ Blow bubbles and suggest that the children chase the bubbles.

Special Event
○ Invite the children to put on a talent show.

Writing
○ Print *I like* _____ on sheets of drawing paper. Provide a basket of picture cards or a basket of concrete items, such as an apple, a book, blocks, beads, and other familiar items. Encourage the children to use the picture cards or concrete items to fill in the blanks.

Home Connection

○ Suggest that children interview their family members regarding things they like to do. When children return to school discuss the information they learned.

I Wish I Were

Vocabulary

bar
click
cookie
crumb
juicy
little
orange
radio
tummy
wish

Theme Connections

Humor
Make-Believe

(Tune: If You're Happy and You
    Know It)
Oh, I wish I were a little juicy
    orange,
Juicy orange.
Oh, I wish I were a little juicy
    orange,
Juicy orange.
I'd go squirty, squirty, squirty
Over everybody's shirty.
Oh, I wish I were a little juicy
    orange,
Juicy orange.

Oh, I wish I were a little bar of
    soap,
Bar of soap.
Oh, I wish I were a little bar of
    soap,
Bar of soap.
For I'd slippy and I'd slidy

Over everybody's hidey.
Oh, I wish I were a little bar of
    soap,
Bar of soap.

Oh, I wish I were a little cookie
    crumb,
Cookie crumb.
Oh, I wish I were a little cookie
    crumb,
Cookie crumb.
I'd go crumby, crumby, crumby
Over everybody's tummy.
Oh, I wish I were a little cookie
    crumb,
Cookie crumb.

Oh, I wish I were a little radio,
    radio.
Oh, I wish I were a little radio,
    radio.
I'd go (static noise, click).

Did You Know?

❍ It is often assumed that young children confuse fantasy and reality. New
    research suggests that children have a more developed appreciation of the
    boundary between fantasy and reality than is often supposed (Wooley,
    2004). Sixty-seven percent of three-year-olds and seventy-three percent of
    four-year-olds were able to understand the difference between real and
    make-believe, and the difference between wishes and reality.
    Wooley, Sharon T. British Journal of Developmental Psychology, Volume
    22, Number 2, June 2004, pp. 293-310(18)

❍ See pages 31 and 34 for information about the value of humor.

Literacy Links

Listening
❍ Read "I Wish I Had a Dinosaur" (page 100).

wish

Oral Language

○ Lead the children in a discussion of *real* and *make-believe*. *What are some wishes that might be make-believe? What wishes could be real?*

○ Teach the children the American Sign Language sign for *wish*.

○ Talk with the children about wishes. *What things do you wish for? Did you make a wish on your birthday candles?* **Note**: Birthdays are not celebrated in the same way in all cultures. Be aware of and sensitive to cultural differences.

Print Awareness/Comprehension

○ Brainstorm a list of things people use to make wishes, such as stars, pennies, birthday candles, wishbones, and four-leaf clovers. Explain to the children that people make wishes at certain times.

Curriculum Connections

Dramatic Play

○ Provide birthday props, such as hats, streamers, presents, and playdough for shaping a cake and birthday candles. Invite the children to pretend they are having a birthday party. Be sure they make a wish when they blow out the birthday cake candles.

Games

○ Hide pennies for the children to find. Suggest that they make a wish when they find a penny.

Special Needs Adaptation: Adapt this for children with motor difficulties by taking three paper cups and turning each one upside down. Place a penny under one and move the cups around. Invite the child to point to the cup where she thinks the penny is hidden.

Language

○ Display things people make wishes on, such as stars (cut out one from poster board), pennies, birthday candles, wishbones, and four-leaf clovers. Encourage the children to make a wish on one of the items.

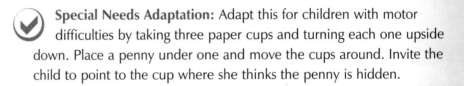

Book Corner

The Amazing Bone
by William Steig
*I Wish that I Had
Duck Feet!* by
Dr. Seuss
*Sylvester and the
Magic Pebble* by
William Steig

Outdoors

○ Encourage the children to look for four-leaf clovers.

Sand and Water Play

○ Place sand and 10-12 granules of rock salt in the sand table to represent stars. Provide sieves for the children to use to find the stars. Have them make a wish on the stars when they find them.

○ Give the children small bars of soap to play with. *Do the bars of soap go "slippy and slidy"?* **Note:** Make sure children do not get the soap in their eyes.

Snack

○ Serve orange wedges and cookies for snack. *Do the oranges go "squirty, squirty, squirty"? Do the cookies "crumby, crumby, crumby" on everybody's tummy?*

Writing

○ Have the children dictate a wish to you. Encourage them to illustrate their wishes.

Home Connection

○ Suggest that children talk with their family members about wishes they may have. Discuss family wishes when the children return to school.

This Little Light of Mine

Chorus:
This little light of mine,
I'm gonna let it shine.
This little light of mine,
I'm gonna let it shine.
This little light of mine,
I'm gonna let it shine.
Let it shine,
Let it shine,
Let it shine.

Hide it under a bushel? No!
I'm gonna let it shine.
Hide it under a bushel? No!
I'm gonna let it shine.
Hide it under a bushel? No!
I'm gonna let it shine.
Let it shine,
Let it shine,
Let it shine.

(Chorus)

Playing with my friends!? Yes!
I'm gonna let it shine.
Singing silly songs!? Yes!
I'm gonna let it shine.
Bouncing rubber balls!? Yes!
I'm gonna let it shine.
Let it shine,
Let it shine,
Let it shine.

(Chorus)

Building with the blocks!? Yes!
I'm gonna let it shine.
Looking at good books!? Yes!
I'm gonna let it shine.
Dancing in my socks!? Yes!
I'm gonna let it shine.
Let it shine,
Let it shine,
Let it shine.

(Chorus)

Vocabulary

bushel
hide
light
little
mine
shine

Theme Connections

Me
Things I Can Do

Did You Know?

○ Light travels through gases, liquids, and some solids. The rate of speed light travels through things depends on the density of the item.

○ Without light we would be unable to see.

○ Without the light of the sun we could not stay warm enough to live. We would have no food to eat or oxygen to breathe because there would be no plant life to supply food and oxygen.

○ In 1704, Sir Isaac Newton discovered that white light is made up of all the colors of light. Before Newton's discovery the common thought was that all colors were made up of lightness and darkness. Scientist believed that white light was created by the absence of darkness. Newton used a prism to prove his theory. He was able to separate the each of the colors made by the prism and then mix them together to create a pure white light. White light is the result of all the colors of the rainbow being mixed together.

Literacy Links

Comprehension/Print Awareness

○ Make a list of ways to stop light, such as covering a flashlight with a box, pulling down a window shade, or standing in front of the light.

○ Challenge the children to make up additional verses to the song using some of the things they listed as making them feel good, such as sharing with my friends at school, helping mom and dad at home, or singing all my favorite songs (see the Oral Language activity). Print the new verses on chart paper so the children can see their words in writing. For example:

Sharing with my friends at school
I'm gonna let it shine.
Sharing with my friends at school,
I'm gonna let it shine,
Sharing with my friends at school,
I'm gonna let it shine,
Let it shine! Let it shine! Let it shine!

Oral Language

○ Talk with the children about the things that make them feel happy. Talk about being kind to others as part of those things. Explain that when we feel happy we "shine."

○ Teach the children the American Sign Language sing for *light* (page 116).

Phonological Awareness

○ Have the children brainstorm more words that rhyme with *mine* and *shine*.

Curriculum Connections

Art

○ Provide drawing paper and crayons. Encourage the children to draw a picture of something that they do well or that makes them feel happy.

Discovery

○ Provide a flashlight and items that the children can shine the light onto, such as a mirror, foil, black paper, cardboard, cellophane, and other materials. *Which things reflect the light? Which things does the light shine through? Which things does the light shine on?*

○ Shine a flashlight through a funnel. *What happens to the light?* Shine a light through a sieve. *What happens to the light?*

Book Corner

Games

○ Hide a light in the classroom. Turn off the rest of the lights and encourage the children to find the hidden light. Continue playing the game, hiding the light in places where it is more and more difficult to find.

Music and Movement

○ Provide a light source and invite the children to dance between the light source and a wall to create shadow dancers.

Science

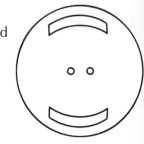

○ Cover several flashlights with colored cellophane and let the children experiment with blending colored light. *What happens when red, blue, and green light are mixed?*

○ Make a strobe light. Cut two 1" x 2" slots, opposite each other, on a pizza cardboard. Punch two small holes near the center of the pizza cardboard. Use twisty ties to attach the pizza cardboard to a handheld beater. Position a flashlight so it will shine through one of the slots. Turn off the classroom lights and start the mixer. Invite the children to dance in the strobe light. Position the strobe light near a source of running water. Turn on the light and turn on the water. *What do you see?* (The light reflects off the water and creates a "light show.")

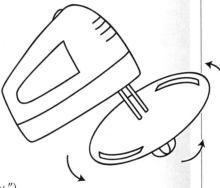

✓ **Special Needs Adaptation:** Some children with seizure disorder should never be exposed to a strobe light, as it can trigger a seizure. In addition, children with autism often do not react well to flashing lights. Instead of a strobe light, invite the children to make shadows using a lamp or flashlight.

Writing

○ Provide a Lite Brite®. Design dots that outline the letters in *shine* on a sheet of paper to place over the Lite Brite screen. Invite the children to punch out the dots.

Home Connection

○ Suggest that the children interview their family members about ways they "let their light shine."

Evan's Bathtub Song

by Richele Bartkowiak

Vocabulary

bath
bath time
bathtub
bubbles
clean
scrub
shampoo
smell
splashin'
splishin'
washcloth
watching

Theme Connections

Bath Time
Me

(Tune: Rock-a-Bye Baby)
Splishin' and a-splashin'
In the bathtub.
When we take a bath
We clean and we scrub.
We use our washcloths
And a little shampoo,
And when it's all over
We smell good as new.

Splishin' and a-splashin'
That's what we do.
Don't forget Ducky
He likes it too.
Watching the bubbles
Dance in the tub,
Oh, how we love bath time,
Rub-a-dub-dub!

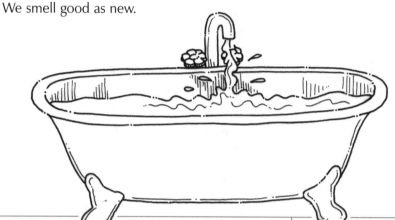

Did You Know?

○ A rubber duck, or rubber duckie, is a toy duck made of rubber or rubber-like material such as vinyl plastic. Today, most rubber ducks are made out of vinyl plastic. It is designed to float, so it is often played with in a bathtub. However, not everyone uses rubber ducks as bath toys. Some people like to have them as a decoration for a locker or bedroom.

○ It is unknown when the first rubber duck was manufactured, but squeak toys have been around since the late 1800s.

○ The yellow rubber duck has achieved an iconic status in American pop culture. In the United States, the rubber duck is often symbolically linked to bathing, bathtubs, and young children.

Literacy Links

bath

Oral Language

❍ Talk about bath time with the children. *When do you take your bath? Do you use bubble bath? Do you have toys in the tub? Which toy is your favorite? Who helps you with your bath? What are the steps in taking a bath?*

❍ Teach the children the American Sign Language sign for *bath*.

Phonological Awareness

❍ Print *splishing* and *splashing* on chart paper. Discuss the meaning of the words. Explain that both words are *onomatopoeic* words—words that sound like the sound they are describing. *What do the words* splishing *and* splashing *describe? What other sounds does water make?*

❍ Encourage the children to think of words that rhyme with *ducky*.

❍ Print *rub-a-dub-dub* on chart paper. Discuss the rhyming of *rub* and *dub*. Ask the children to identify the letters in *rub* and *dub*. *Which letters are the same?* Teach the children "Rub-a-Dub-Dub, Three Men in a Tub."

Rub-a-Dub-Dub, Three Men in a Tub
Rub-a-dub-dub, three men in a tub,
And who do you think they be?
The butcher, the baker, the candlestick maker,
Turn them out, knaves all three.

Curriculum Connections

Discovery

❍ Give the children small bars of soap to play with in the sand and water table. Remind children not to put soapy hands on their mouths or eyes. *How does soap feel on your hands? Does the soap sink or float? Do you like the way the soap smells?* **Allergy warning**: Check for allergies before allowing the children to play with soap.

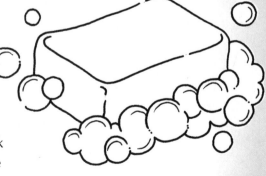

Dramatic Play

❍ Provide baby dolls, a tub of sudsy water, a washcloth, empty shampoo and soft soap bottles, and a rubber duck.

Fine Motor

❍ Provide a bowl of soapy water and hand beaters. Encourage the children to beat the soapy water until bubbles spill over the side of the bowl.

Language

❍ Photocopy the Bath Time Sequence Cards (page 112). Color them, cut them out, and laminate them. Have the children sequence the cards in the correct order to show the steps in taking a bath.

Math

❍ Provide washcloths. Show the children how to fold the washcloths by folding the cloth in half and then in half again. Discuss the folds. Crease a folded washcloth and then open it so that children can see the cloth has four equal sections.

Music

❍ Teach the children "Annie Mae" (page 97). Discuss the improbability of going down the drain at the end of bath time.

Outdoors

❍ Blow bubbles for the children to chase.

Sand and Water Play

❍ Provide rubber ducks for the children to play with.

Writing

❍ Print *ducky* on chart paper. Provide magnetic letters and encourage the children to copy the word.

Home Connection

❍ Send home a set of Bath Time Sequence Cards (page 112) with each child. Encourage the children to use the cards to discuss bath time routines with their family members. They can also use the cards when they take a bath to see if their bath time routine matches the one on the sequence cards.

Book Corner

Bathtime, Maisy! by Lucy Cousins

Bathtime Piggywiggy by Christyan Fox

Elmo Wants a Bath by Joseph Mathieu

The Fish Is Me!: Bathtime Rhymes by Neil Philip

Why Is Soap so Slippery? And Other Bathtime Questions by Catherine Ripley

Skidamarink

Skidamarink a dink a dink,
Skidamarink a doo,
I love you.
Skidamarink a dink a dink,
Skidamarink a doo,
I love you.

I love you in the morning
And in the afternoon,
I love you in the evening
And underneath the moon.
Oh, Skidamarink a dink a dink,
Skidamarink a doo,
I love you!

Vocabulary

afternoon
evening
love
moon
morning
underneath

Theme Connections

Family
Friends
Humor

Did You Know?

○ Every February 14th, loved ones exchange candy, flowers, and gifts, all in the name of St. Valentine. But who is this mysterious saint and why do we celebrate this holiday? There are two legends explaining the origin of Valentine's Day.

○ Legend #1: In the year 269 A.D., Roman Emperor Claudius II had a difficult time getting soldiers to join the military because they did not want to leave their loves or families. So, he cancelled all marriages and engagements in Rome! Saint Valentine, who was a priest in Rome, defied Claudius and continued to perform marriages for young lovers in secret. Claudius discovered what Valentine was doing, put him in prison, and sentenced him to die. While in prison, Valentine fell in love with a young girl, who visited him during his confinement. Before his death on the 14th day of February, it is alleged that he wrote her a letter, which he signed, "From your Valentine." In 496 A.D., Pope Gelasius set aside February 14th to honor St. Valentine.

○ Legend #2: In ancient Rome, February 14th was a holiday to honor Juno. Juno was the queen of the Roman gods and goddesses. The Romans also knew her as the goddess of women and marriage. February 15th the Feast of Lupercalia began. Although the lives of young boys and girls were strictly separate, on the eve of the festival of Lupercalia, the names of Roman girls were written on slips of paper and placed into jars. Each young man would draw a girl's name from the jar. They would be partners for the duration of the festival. Sometimes the pairing of the children lasted an entire year, and often, they would fall in love and would later marry.

○ No matter which legend you believe, the outcome is the same—Valentine became a patron saint and the custom of handwritten greetings was begun.

○ In the United States, Miss Esther Howland is given credit for sending the first Valentine cards. Commercial valentines were introduced in the 1800's.

Literacy Links

Oral Language

○ Teach the children the American Sign Language sign for *I love you*.

○ Print *Skidamarink* on chart paper. Ask the children what the word means. Their guesses might be quite creative (and cute!), but eventually the children will discover that it is a nonsense word. Discuss other nonsense words, such as *doodley-do*, *thinga-majig*, and *razamataz*.

○ Talk with the children about the people they love.

> **Special Needs Adaptation:** Ask the child's family to send pictures of family members to school. Talk to the child about her family and ask her to point to each family member. Talk about things the child can do to show her family that she loves them.

I love you

Phonological Awareness

○ Encourage children to think of a number that rhymes with *you*. Challenge them to think of a color that rhymes with *you*. Invite them to make a list of words that rhyme with *you*.

Segmentation

○ Have the children clap the words *I love you*. Have them clap the syllables in each word. *Does anything change?*

Curriculum Connections

Art

○ Provide cutout hearts in a variety of sizes and colors. Encourage the children to use the hearts to make a heart collage.

○ Suggest that the children use paper, paintbrushes, and red tempera paint to paint hearts.

○ Provide materials for children to make "Skidamarink I Love You" cards for their family members.

Book Corner

Discovery

○ Provide an empty paper towel tube to use as a stethoscope. Encourage the children to use the paper towel tube to listen to each others' heartbeat. (The first child puts one end of the paper towel tube to his ear and the second child holds the other end against her chest.) Suggest that the second child do some jumping jacks and then the first child should listen again. Does he notice any difference in what he hears?

Fine Motor

○ Give the children playdough and heart-shaped cookie cutters. Provide decorative beads, buttons, and confetti. Invite the children to make pretend heart cookies and then decorate them.

Gross Motor

○ Use masking tape to print *I love you* in giant letters on the floor. Have the children walk the letters while balancing a paper heart on their head.

Language

○ Cut large hearts from construction paper. Laminate them and then cut them into puzzle pieces. Have the children "repair" the broken hearts. Discuss the meaning of broken heart.

Music

○ Sing songs about loving someone, such as "You Are My Sunshine" and "A Bicycle Built for Two."

Writing

○ Print *Skidamarink* on chart paper. Provide both magnetic letters and markers. Invite the children to copy the nonsense word.

Home Connection

○ Send home the "Skidamarink I Love You Cards" that the children made for their family members.

More Learning and Fun

Songs

Annie Mae

Annie Mae, where are you going?
Up the stairs to take a bath.
Annie Mae with legs like toothpicks
And a neck like a giraffe.
Annie Mae stepped in the bathtub.
Annie Mae pulled out the plug.
Oh my goodness!
Oh my soul!
There goes Annie Mae down that hole.
Annie Mae?
Annie Mae?
Gurgle, gurgle, glug.

Be Kind to Your Web-Footed Friends

(Tune: Stars and Stripes Forever)
Be kind to your web-footed friends,
For a duck may be somebody's mother.
Be kind to the birds in the swamp,
For the weather is very damp
Oh, you may think that this is the end,
Well, it is!

The Donut Song

(Tune: Turkey in the Straw)
Oh, I ran around the corner,
And I ran around the block
I ran right in to the baker shop.
I grabbed me a donut,
Right out of the grease,
And I handed the lady
A five-cent piece.
She looked at the nickel,

And she looked at me.
She said, "This nickel
Ain't no good to me.
There's a hole in the nickel,
And it goes right through."
Said I, "There's a hole in your donut, too!
Thanks for the donut. Good-bye!" *(more said than sung)*

Here We Go 'Round the Mulberry Bush

Here we go 'round the mulberry bush,
The mulberry bush, the mulberry bush.
Here we go 'round the mulberry bush,
So early in the morning.

These are the chores we'll do this week,
Do this week, do this week.
These are the chores we'll do this week,
So early every morning.

This is the way we wash our clothes,
Wash our clothes, wash our clothes.
This is the way we wash our clothes,
So early Monday morning.

This is the way we iron our clothes...So early
    Tuesday morning.
This is the way we scrub the floor...So early
    Wednesday morning.
This is the way we mend our clothes...So early
    Thursday morning.
This is the way we sweep the floor...So early
    Friday morning.
This is the way we bake our bread... So early
    Saturday morning.
This is the way we get dressed up...So early
    Sunday morning.

Here we go 'round the mulberry bush,
The mulberry bush, the mulberry bush.
Here we go 'round the mulberry bush,
So early in the morning.

If You're Happy, Laugh Out Loud
adapted by Pam Schiller

If you're happy and you know it, laugh out loud.
    (ha, ha, ha)
If you're happy and you know it, laugh out loud.
    (ha, ha, ha)
If you're happy and you know it,
Then your laugh can help you show it.
If you're happy and you know it, laugh our loud.
    (ha, ha, ha)

If you're sad and you know it, say, "I'm sad."
    ("I'm sad!")
If you're sad and you know it, say, "I'm sad."
    ("I'm sad!")
If you're sad and you know it,
Then your words can help you show it.
If you're sad and you know it, say, "I'm sad."
    ("I'm sad!")

If you're angry and you know it, stomp your feet.
    (stomp, stomp, stomp)
If you're angry and you know it, stomp your feet.
    (stomp, stomp, stomp)
If you're angry and you know it,
Then your feet can help you show it.
If you're angry and you know it, stomp your feet.
    (stomp, stomp, stomp)

If you're surprised and you know it, say, "Yippee!"
    ("yippee!")
If you're surprised and you know it, say, "Yippee!"
    ("yippee!")
If you're surprised and you know it,
Then your words can help you show it.
If you're surprised and you know it, say, "Yippee!"
    ("yippee!")

The Iguana in Lavender Socks
by Pam Schiller
(Tune: On Top of Old Smokey)

On top of a hillside,
All covered with rocks,
There lives an iguana,
With lavender socks.

She bathes in the sunshine
And cools in the lake.
She dines on tamales
And fly-covered cake.

When she is happy
She plays her guitar.
And all the iguanas
Think she's a rock star.

They dance on the hillside
And over the rocks.
They dance with the iguana
In lavender socks.

They dance thru the daylight
And into the night
Those dancing iguanas
A humorous sight.

I love that iguana,
She's totally cool.
I wish that iguana
Would dance to my school.

One Black Bear
(Tune: Battle Hymn of the Republic)
As one black bear backed up the hill,
The other black bear backed down, *(repeat the
    lines four times)*

Chorus:
Glory, glory, how peculiar,
Glory, glory, how peculiar,
Glory, glory, how peculiar,
As one black bear backed up the hill,
The other black bear backed down.

As one fresh fish flipped into the fire,
The other fresh fish flipped out. (repeat the lines
    four times)

(Chorus)

As one purple porpoise popped in the pool,
The other purple porpoise popped out.
    (repeat the lines four times)

(Chorus)

As one eager eagle eased under the eave,
The other eager eagle eased out. (repeat the
    lines four times)

(Chorus)

Rockabye, Baby

Rockabye, baby,
In the tree top
When the wind blows ,
The cradle will rock.
When the bough breaks,
The cradle will fall,
And down will come baby,
Cradle and all.

The Song That Never Ends

This is the song that never ends,
It just goes on and on, my friend.
Someone started singing it not knowing
    what it was
And they'll go on singing it forever just because
This is the song that never ends,
It just goes on and on, my friend.
Someone started singing it not knowing
    what it was
And they'll go on singing it forever because
This is the song that never ends...
(Repeat until you or someone else tires
    of hearing the song!)

This Is the Way We Wash Our Face
  by Pam Schiller
(Tune: Here We Go 'Round the Mulberry Bush)
This is the way we wash our face,
Scrub our cheeks,
Scrub our ears.
This is the way we wash our face,
Until we're squeaky clean.

This is the way we dry our face,
Gently pat, Gently rub.
This is the way we dry our face
Now we're clean and dry.

Chants and Rhymes

After My Bath

After my bath I try, try, try
To rub with a towel till I'm dry, dry, dry.
Hands to dry, and fingers and toes,
And two wet legs and a shiny nose.
Just think how much less time it'd take
If I were a dog and could shake, shake, shake!

A-Root-Chy-Cha

Hands up! (children echo and do motion)
Wrists together! (children echo and do motion)
A-root-chy-cha, a-root-chy-cha, a-root-chy-cha
CHA!
A-root-chy-cha, a-root-chy-cha, a-root-chy-cha
CHA!
Hands up! (echo)
Wrists together! (echo)
Elbows in! (echo) (keep adding the motion)
A-root-chy-cha, a-root-chy-cha, a-root-chy-cha
CHA!
A-root-chy-cha, a-root-chy-cha, a-root-chy-cha
CHA!
Hands up! (echo)
Wrists together! (echo)
Elbows in! (echo)
Head back! (echo)
A-root-chy-cha, a-root-chy-cha, a-root-chy-cha
CHA!

A-root-chy-cha, a-root-chy-cha, a-root-chy-cha
CHA!
*(Keep going back to the beginning, adding one
motion each time and doing the "root-chy-cha"
chorus. During the chorus, the children are moving
to the beat.)*
Additional verses:
Knees together....
Toes together....
Bottom out....
Eyes closed....
Tongue out.....

I Can, Can You? by Pam Schiller

I can put my hands up high. Can you?
I can wink my eye. Can you?
I can stick out my tongue. Can you?
I can nod my head. Can you?
I can kiss my toe. Can you?
I can pull on my ear. Can you?
I can wrinkle my nose. Can you?
I can give myself a great big hug. Can you?
And if I give my hug to you, will you give yours
   to me?

I Help My Family by Pam Schiller

(suit actions to words)
I help my family when I can.
I fold the clothes.
I feed the dog.
I turn on the hose.

I crack the eggs.
I ice the cake.
Then I help eat
The good things we make.

I Wish I Had a Dinosaur by Pam Schiller

I wish I had a dinosaur
That I could call my own.
I'd take him with me everywhere,
He'd never be alone.

A football field would be his bed
A swimming pool his tub.
I'd need a ladder to reach his head,
A blanket for a rub.

I'd need bushels of leafy food,
A tree for playing fetch,
Bundles of cloth to make his clothes,
And a basketball for catch.

I'd call him Dino De Dandee,
He'd be my bestest friend.
When you saw him—you'd see me,
That's how close we would be.

I wish I had a dinosaur
To call my very own.
I'd take him with me everywhere,
I'd never be alone.

Pairs

A pair of eyes here on my face.
A pair of eyebrows right in place.
A pair of ears to hear a sound.
A pair of legs to run around.
A pair of shoulders strong and wide.
A pair of hips, one on each side.
A pair of ankles near my feet,
A pair of hands all washed and neat.

Thelma Thumb

(move thumb as directed)
Thelma Thumb is up and Thelma Thumb is down.
Thelma Thumb is dancing all around the town.
Dance her on your shoulders, dance her on your
   head.
Dance her on your knees and tuck her into bed.

Names for other fingers—Phillip Pointer, Terry Tall,
   Richie Ring, and Baby Finger, Finger Family and
   dance them on other body parts.

What Makes Me Laugh? by Pam Schiller
Bubbles in the air.
My fingers in your hair.
Silly songs we sing.
Balloons on a string.
Jack in the box.
And spinning tops.
Tickles on my toes.
Kisses on my nose.
What makes you laugh?

Fingerplays

Five Little Fingers
One little finger standing on its own. (hold up index finger)
Two little fingers, now they're not alone. (hold up middle finger)
Three little fingers happy as can be. (hold up ring finger)
Four little fingers go walking down the street. (hold up all fingers)
Five little fingers. This one is a thumb. (hold up four fingers and thumb)
Wave bye-bye 'cause now we are done. (wave bye-bye)

Five Wooden Soldiers
(Hold up five fingers. Starting with the little finger, bend each finger down as the rhyme progresses.)
Five wooden soldiers standing in a row
Look out! Look out! Down they go.
Down goes the little man.
Down goes ring man.
Down goes middle man.
Down goes pointer.
Down goes thumbkin.
All five soldiers, sleeping 'til dawn.

I Have a Little Wagon
I have a little wagon (hold hand out palm up)
It goes everywhere with me. (move had around)
I can pull it (pull hand toward you)
I can push it (push hand away from you)
I can turn it upside down. (turn hand upside down)

When I Was One
When I was one I was so small, (hold up one finger)
I could not speak a word at all. (shake head)
When I was two, I learned to talk, (hold up two fingers)
I learned to sing, I learned to walk. (point to mouth and feet)
When I was three, I grew and grew. (hold up two fingers)
Now I am four and so are you! (hold up four fingers)

Stories

The Many Faces of Me by Pam Schiller
(Action Story)
My mother says I wear many faces.
When I am happy I look like this. (turn around and smile)
When I am mad I look like this. (turn around and look angry)
When I am sad I look like this. (turn around and look sad)
When I am confused I look like this. (turn around and look confused)
When I daydream I look like this. (turn around and look pensive)
When my grandmother comes to visit I look like this. (turn opposite direction and smile)
When my brother knocks down my sandcastle I look like this. (turn and look angry)
When I can't have a second helping of ice cream I look like this. (turn and look sad)
When I can't find my shoes I look like this. (turn and look confused)
When I am thinking about summer vacation I look like this. (turn and look pensive)
How many faces do you have? (point to another child)

What Makes Me Laugh?
by Pam Schiller (Listening Story)

You make me laugh!
You stick out your tongue—I jump with joy.
You make a funny face—I can barely
    contain myself.
You play a game with me—I wiggle and giggle.
You wear a goofy hat—I'm in awesome wonder.
We make silly faces in the mirror—I shake
    with delight.
You talk to me—I babble and coo and smile
You tickle me—I laugh out loud.
You give me a hug—I smile from the inside out.
You make me laugh!

Fun Facts About Me, My Family and Friends

The Body
○ The highest recorded "sneeze speed" is 165 km (102 miles) per hour.
○ The heart beats about three billion times in the average person's lifetime.
○ The average cough comes out of your mouth at 60 miles (96.5 km) per hour.
○ When you sneeze, all your bodily functions stop, including your heart.
○ The average human head weighs about eight pounds.
○ In the average lifetime, a person will walk the equivalent of 5 times around the equator.
○ The length of the finger dictates how fast the fingernail grows. The nail on your middle finger grows the fastest, and, on average, your toenails grow twice as slow as your fingernails.
○ Your ears and nose continue to grow throughout your entire life.
○ The most sensitive cluster of nerves is at the base of the spine.
○ The human body is comprised of 80% water.
○ The average human will shed 40 pounds of skin in a lifetime.
○ Babies are born with 300 bones; adults have 206.
○ Human thighbones are stronger than concrete.

Sleep
○ Sleep experts say most adults need between seven and nine hours of sleep each night for optimum performance, health and safety. When we don't get adequate sleep, we accumulate a sleep debt that can be difficult to "pay back" if it becomes too big. The resulting sleep deprivation has been linked to health problems such as obesity and high blood pressure, negative mood and behavior, decreased productivity, and safety issues in the home, on the job, and on the road.
○ Snoring is harmless for most people. However, it can be a symptom of a life-threatening sleep disorder called sleep apnea, especially if it is accompanied by severe daytime sleepiness. Sleep apnea is characterized by pauses in breathing that prevent air from flowing into or out of a sleeping person's airways. People with sleep apnea awaken frequently during the night gasping for breath. The breathing pauses reduce blood oxygen levels, can strain the heart and cardiovascular system, and increase the risk of cardiovascular disease.
○ Difficulty falling asleep is but one of four symptoms generally associated with insomnia. The others include waking up too early and not being able to fall back asleep, frequent awakenings, and waking up feeling unrested. Insomnia can be a symptom of a sleep disorder or other medical or psychological/psychiatric problem, and can often be treated. According to the National Sleep Foundation's 2002 Sleep in America poll, 58 percent of adults in this country reported at least one symptom of insomnia in the past year. When insomnia symptoms occur more than a few times a week and impact a person's daytime functions, the symptoms should be discussed with a doctor or other health care provider.

National Sleep Foundation, Washington, DC

Recipes

Magic Crystal Garden Recipe
Ingredients
6 tablespoons salt
6 tablespoons liquid bluing (see Note)
6 tablespoons water
1 tablespoon ammonia
food coloring (optional)

Combine salt, bluing, water, and ammonia. Safety Warning: Only adults should handle ammonia. Pour over small pieces of rock or coal in a shallow glass or china bowl. Drip food coloring on top, if desired. Crystals will soon begin to grow. Add water occasionally to keep crystals growing. You'll probably want to place dish on a tray or wooden board as crystals grow over the sides of the bowl. **Note:** Liquid bluing can be found in most markets with the laundry soaps and products. One popular brand is Mrs. Stewart's Liquid Bluing and is used as a laundry whitener.

Scented Playdough Recipe #1
3 cups flour
1 ½ cups salt
3 tablespoons massage oil
2 tablespoons cream of tartar
3 cups water

Combine all ingredients. Cook over very low heat until mixture is no longer sticky to the touch.

Scented Playdough Recipe #2
1 package Kool-Aid
1 cup water
1 teaspoon baby oil
1 cup flour
½ cup salt
2 teaspoons cream of tartar

Mix Kool-Aid and water on stove over medium heat until steam rises. Add baby oil and stir. Mix together remaining dry ingredients. Gradually add to heated liquids and stir until a mashed potato consistency is achieved. Remove from stove; place playdough on wax paper and knead until smooth. Allow to cool.

Baggie Ice Cream Recipe
(makes one serving)
½ cup milk
1 tablespoon sugar
¼ teaspoon vanilla
small zipper-closure plastic bag
large zipper-closure plastic bag
3 tablespoons rock salt

Place the milk, sugar, and vanilla in the small bag and seal it. Place the small bag, rock salt, and ice cubes in the large bag and seal. Shake.

Friendship Donuts Rebus Recipe

Friendship Donut Recipe

1.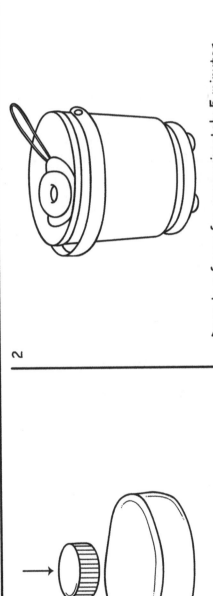

   Give each child a refrigerator biscuit and a bottle cap to punch a hole in the middle of the biscuit.

2.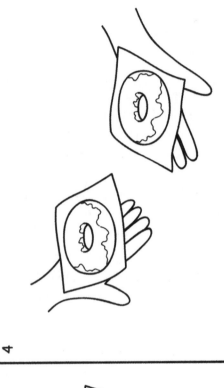

   Drop in a fryer for approximately 5 minutes. (WARNING: Keep children away from fryer. Only the teacher should drop biscuits in the grease.)

3. Powdered Sugar

   Let the children dust their donut with powdered sugar.

4.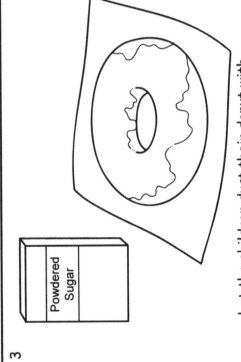

   Have the children exchange donuts with a friend before eating.

Happy Face Rebus Recipe

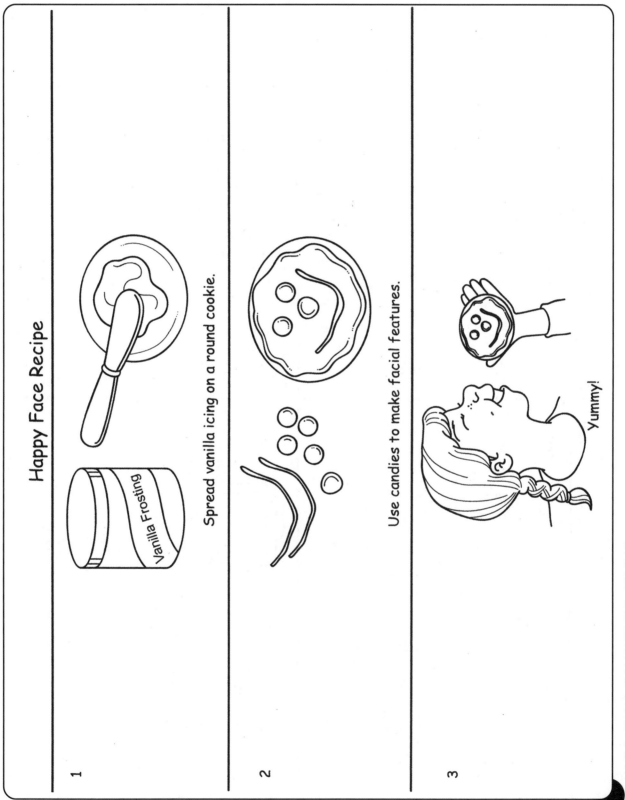

Happy Face Recipe

1. Vanilla Frosting

   Spread vanilla icing on a round cookie.

2. Use candies to make facial features.

3. Yummy!

Catalina Magnalina Shakalina Rebus Recipe

Catalina Magnalina Shakalina Recipe

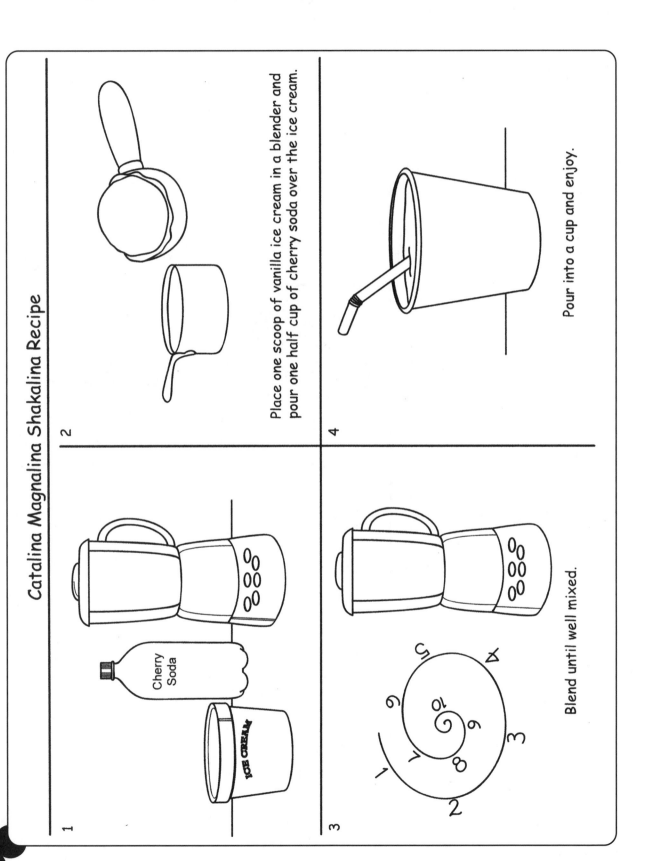

1

Cherry Soda

ICE CREAM

2

Place one scoop of vanilla ice cream in a blender and pour one half cup of cherry soda over the ice cream.

3

Blend until well mixed.

4

Pour into a cup and enjoy.

Making Butter Rebus Recipe

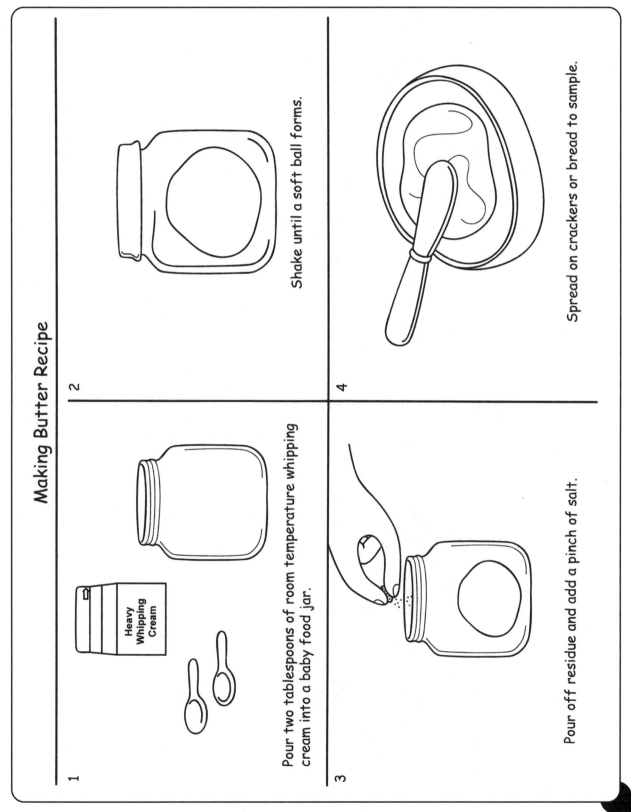

Making Butter Recipe

1. Pour two tablespoons of room temperature whipping cream into a baby food jar.

2. Shake until a soft ball forms.

3. Pour off residue and add a pinch of salt.

4. Spread on crackers or bread to sample.

Heavy Whipping Cream

Finger Puppets

Happy Face Match Up

Pattern Cards

Pattern Cards

Bath Time Sequence Cards

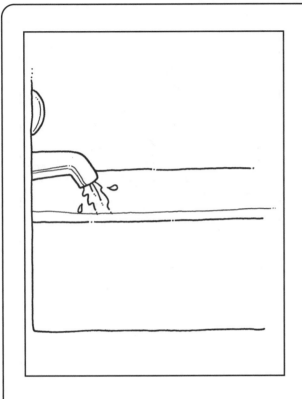

Things I Like to Do Cards

Things I Like to Do Cards

American Sign Language Signs

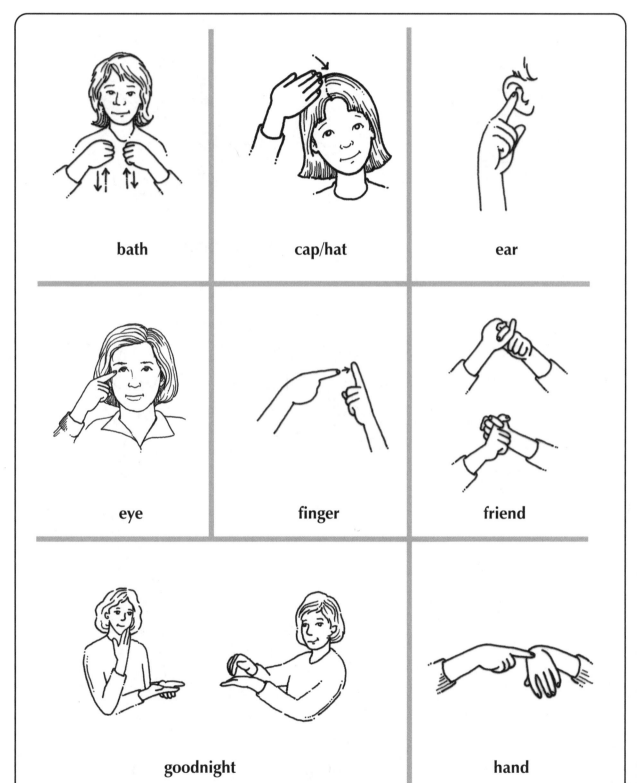

bath

cap/hat

ear

eye

finger

friend

goodnight

hand

American Sign Language Signs

happy

Happy Birthday

head

hello

I love you

Point to knee.

knee

laugh

light

American Sign Language Signs

magic

mittens

mouth

nose

sad

shoulder

smile

toe

wish

References and Bibliography

Bulloch, K. 2003. *The mystery of modifying: Creative solutions*. Huntsville, TX: Education Service Center, Region VI.

Cavallaro, C. & M. Haney. 1999. *Preschool inclusion*. Baltimore, MD: Paul H. Brookes Publishing Company.

Gray, T. and S. Fleischman. Dec. 2004-Jan. 2005. "Research matters: Successful strategies for English language learners." *Educational Leadership*, 62, 84-85.

Hanniford, C. 1995. *Smart moves: Why learning is not all in your head*. Arlington, VA: Great Ocean Publications, p. 146.

Keller, M. 2004. "Warm weather boosts mood, broadens the mind." Ann Arbor, MI : Post Doctoral Study: The University of Michigan.

LeDoux, J. 1993. "Emotional memory systems in the brain." *Behavioral and Brain Research,* 58.

Theme Index

Children's Book Index

Index